THE HATHA YOGA PRADIPIKA

Swami Swatmarama

Translated into English by

PANCHAM SINH

pacps

Pacific Publishing Studio

Published in the United States by Pacific Publishing Studio.

www.PacPS.com

ISBN-13: 978-1463727918

ISBN-10: 1463727917

CONTENTS

INTRODUCTION

There exists at present a good deal of misconception with regard to the practices of the Haṭha Yoga. People easily believe in the stories told by those who themselves heard them second hand, and no attempt is made to find out the truth by a direct reference to any good treatise. It is generally believed that the six practices, (षट्कर्म) in Haṭha Yoga are compulsory on the student and that besides being dirty, they are fraught with danger to the practiser. This is not true, for these practices are necessary only in the existence of impurities in the Nâdis, and not otherwise.

There is the same amount of misunderstanding with regard to the Prâṇâyâma. People put their faith implicitly in the stories told them about the dangers attending the practice, without ever taking the trouble of ascertaining the fact themselves. We have been inspiring and expiring air from our birth, and will continue to do so till death; and this is done without the help of any teacher. Prâṇâyâma is nothing but a properly regulated form of the otherwise irregular and hurried flow of air, without using much force or undue restraint; and if this is accomplished by patiently keeping the flow slow and steady, there can be no danger. It is the impatience for the Siddhis which cause undue pressure on the organs and thereby causes pains in the ears, the eyes, the chest, etc. If the three bandhas (बन्ध) be carefully performed while practising the Prâṇâyâma, there is no possibility of any danger.

There are two classes of students of Yoga: (1) those who study it theoretically; (2) those who combine the theory with practice.

Yoga is of very little use, if studied theoretically. It was never meant for such a study. In its practical form, however, the path of the student is beset with difficulties. The books on Yoga give instructions so far as it is possible to express the methods in words, but all persons, not being careful enough to follow these instructions to the very letter, fail in their object. Such persons require a teacher versed in the practice of Yoga. It is easy to find a teacher who will explain the language of the books, but this is far from being satisfactory. For instance, a Pandit without any knowledge of the science of Materia Medica will explain कंटकारि as कंटकस्यारिः कंटकारिः or an enemy of thorns, *i.e.*, shoes, while it is in reality the name of a medicinal plant, The importance of a practical Yogî as a guide to a student of Yoga cannot be overestimated; and without such a teacher it is next to impossible for him to achieve anything. The methods followed by the founders of the system and followed ever afterwards by their followers, have been wisely and advisedly kept secret; and this is not without a deep meaning. Looking to the gravity of the subject and the practices which have a very close relation with the vital organs of the human body, it is of paramount importance that the instructions should be received by students of ordinary capacity, through a practical teacher only, in order to avoid any possibility of mistake in practice. Speaking broadly, all men are not equally fitted to receive the instructions on equal terms. Man inherits on birth his mental and physical capitals, according to his actions in past births, and has to increase them by manipulation, but there are, even among such, different grades. Hence, one cannot become a Yogî in one incarnation, as says Śri Kṛiṣṇa बहूनांजन्मनामन्ते मामप्रपद्यतिभारत । and again

मनुष्याणां सहस्रेषु कश्चिद्यतति सिद्धये । यततामपिसिद्धानां कश्चिन्मांवेत्ति तत्त्वतः ॥

गीता ॥

There are men who, impelled by the force of their actions of previous births, go headlong and accomplish their liberation in a single attempt; but others have to earn it in their successive births. If the student belongs to one of such souls and being earnest, desires from his heart to get rid of the pains of birth and death, he will find the means too. It is well-known that a true Yogî is above temptations and so to think that he keeps his knowledge secret for selling it to the highest bidder is simply absurd. Yoga is meant for the good of all creatures, and a true Yogî is always desirous of benefitting as many men as possible. But he is not to throw away this precious treasure indiscriminately. He carefully chooses its recipients, and when he finds a true and earnest student, who will not trifle with this knowledge, he never hesitates in placing his valuable treasure at the disposal of the man. What is essential in him is that he should have a real thirst for such knowledge—a thirst which will make him restless till satisfied; the thirst that will make him blind to the world and its enjoyments. He should be, in short, fired with मुमुक्षुत्व or desire for emancipation. To such a one, there is nothing dearer than the accomplishment of this object. A true lover will risk his very life to gain union with his beloved like Tulasîdâs. A true lover will see everywhere, in every direction, in every tree and leaf, in every blade of grass his own beloved. The whole of the world, with all its beauties, is a dreary waste in his eyes, without his beloved. And he will court death, fall into the mouth of a gaping grave, for the sake of his beloved. The student whose heart burns with such intense desire for union with Paraṃâtmâ, is sure to find a teacher, and through him he will surely find Him It is a tried experience that Paraṃâtmâ will try to meet you half way, with the degree of intensity with which you will go to meet Him. Even He Himself will become your guide, direct you on to the road to success, or put you on the track to find a teacher, or lead him to you.

Well has it been said

जिन ढूँढा तिन पाइयां गहरे पानी पैठि । मैं बावरि ढूँढन चली रही किनारे बैठि ॥

It is the half-hearted who fail. They hold their worldly pleasures dearer to their hearts than their God, and therefore He in His turn does not consider them worthy of His favours. Says the Upaniṣad:—

नायमात्मा प्रवचनेन लभ्यो न मेधया न बहुना श्रुतेन । यमेवैष वृणुते तेनलभ्यस्तस्यैष आत्मा विवृणुते तनुस्वाम् ॥

The âtmâ will choose you its abode only if it considers you worthy of such a favour, and not otherwise. It is therefore necessary that one should first make oneself worthy of His acceptance. Having prepared the temple (your heart) well fitted for His installation there, having cleared it of all the impurities which stink and make the place unsuitable for the highest personage to live in, and having decorated it beautifully with objects as befit that Lord of the creation, you need not wait long for Him to adorn this temple of yours which you have taken pains to make it worthy of Him. If you have done all this, He will shine in you in all His glory. In your difficult moments, when you are embarrassed, sit in a contemplative mood, and approach your Parama Guru submissively and refer your difficulties to Him, you are sure to get the proper advice from Him. He is the Guru of the ancients, for He is not limited by Time. He instructed the ancients in bygone times, like a Guru, and if you have been unable to find a teacher in the human form, enter your inner temple and consult this Great Guru who accompanies you everywhere, and ask Him to show you the way. He knows best what is best, for you. Unlike mortal beings, He is beyond the past and the future, will either send one of His agents to guide you or lead you to one and put you on the right track. He is always anxious to teach the earnest seekers, and waits for you to offer Him an opportunity to do so. But if you have not done your duty and prepared yourself worthy of entering His door, and try to gain access to His presence, laden with your unclean burden, stinking with Kama, Krodha, Lobha, and Moha, be sure He will keep you off from Him.

The Âsanas are a means of gaining steadiness of position and help to gain success in contemplation, without any distraction of the mind. If the position be not comfortable, the slightest inconvenience will draw the mind away from the lakśya (aim), and so no peace of mind will be possible till the posture has ceased to cause pain by regular exercise.

Of all the various methods for concentrating the mind, repetition of Praṇava or Ajapâ Jâpa and contemplation on its meaning is the best. It is impossible for the mind to sit idle even for a single moment, and, therefore, in order to keep it well occupied and to keep other antagonistic thoughts from entering it, repetition of Praṇava should be practised. It should be repeated till Yoga Nidrâ is induced which, when experienced, should be encouraged by slackening all the muscles of the body. This will fill the mind with sacred and divine thoughts and will bring about its one-pointedness, without much effort.

Anâhata Nâda is awakened by the exercise of Prâṇâyâma. A couple of weeks' practice with 80 prâṇâyâmas in the morning and the same number in the evening will cause distinct sounds to be heard; and, as the practice will go on increasing, varied sounds become audible to the practiser. By hearing these sounds attentively one gets concentration of the mind, and thence Sahaja Samâdhi. When Yoga sleep is experienced, the student should give himself up to it and make no efforts to check it. By and by, these sounds become subtle and they become less and less intense, so the mind loses its waywardness and becomes calm and docile; and, on this practice becoming well-established, Samâdhi becomes a voluntary act. This is, however, the highest stage and is the lot of the favoured and fortunate few only.

During contemplation one sees, not with his eyes, as he does the objects of the world, various colours, which the writers on Yoga call the colours of the five elements. Sometimes, stars are seen glittering, and lightning flashes in the sky. But these are all fleeting in their nature.

At first these colours are seen in greatly agitated waves which show the unsteady condition of the mind; and as the practice increases and the mind becomes calm, these colour-waves become steady and motionless and appear as one deep ocean of light. This is the ocean in which One should dive and forget the world and become one with his Lord—which is the condition of highest bliss.

Faith in the practices of Yoga, and in one's own powers to accomplish what others have done before, is of great importance to insure speedy success. I mean "faith that will move mountains," will accomplish anything, be it howsoever difficult. There is nothing which cannot be accomplished by practice. Says Śiva in Śiva Saṃhitâ.

अभ्यासाज्जायते सिद्धिरभ्यासान्मोक्षमाप्नुयात् ॥
संविदंलभतेऽभ्यासा द्योगोभ्यासात्प्रवर्तते ।
मुद्राणांसिद्धिरभ्यासा दभ्यासाद्वायुसाधनम् ॥
कालवञ्चनमभ्यासात्तथामृत्युञ्जयोभवेत् ।
वाक्सिद्धिः कामचारित्वं भवेदभ्यासयोगतः ॥ अ० ४ श्लोक ९—११

Through practice success is obtained; through practice one gains liberation.

Perfect consciousness is gained through practice; Yoga is attained through practice; success in mudrâs comes by practice. Through practice is gained success in Prâṇâyâma. Death can be evaded of its prey through practice, and man becomes the conqueror of death by practice. And then let us gird up our loins, and with a firm resolution engage in the practice, having faith in कर्मण्येवाधिकारस्ते मा फलेषु कदाचन, and the success must be ours. May the Almighty Father, be pleased to shower His blessings on those who thus engage in the performance of their duties. Om Siam.

PANCHAM SINH.
AJMER:
31st *January*, 1915.

THE HAṬHA YOGA PRADIPIKA.

हठ-योग-परदीपिका

haṭha-yogha-pradīpikā

CHAPTER 1.

On Âsanas.

|| १ || परथमोपदेशः

|| 1 || prathamopadeśaḥ

शरी-आदि-नाथाय नमो|अस्तु तस्मै
येनोपदिष्हटा हठ-योग-विद्या |
विभ्राजते परोन्नत-राज-योगम
आरोढुमिच्छोरधिरोहिणीव || १ || || १ ||

śrī-ādi-nāthāya namo|astu tasmai
yenopadishṭā haṭha-yogha-vidyā |
vibhrājate pronnata-rāja-yogham
āroḍhumichchoradhirohiṇīva || 1 || || 1 ||

Salutation to Âdinâtha (Śiva) who expounded the knowledge of Haṭha Yoga, which like a staircase leads the aspirant to the high pinnacled Râja Yoga. 1.

परणम्य शरी-गुरुं नाथं सवात्मारामेण योगिना |
केवलं राज-योगाय हठ-विद्योपदिश्यते || २ ||

praṇamya śrī-ghuruṃ nāthaṃ svātmārāmeṇa yoghinā |
kevalaṃ rāja-yoghāya haṭha-vidyopadiśyate || 2 ||

Yogin Swâtmârâma, after saluting first his Gurû Srinâtha explains Haṭha Yoga for the attainment of Raja Yoga. 2.

भरान्त्या बहुमत-धवान्ते राज-योगमजानताम |
हठ-परदीपिकां धत्ते सवात्मारामः कृपाकरः || ३ |

bhrāntyā bahumata-dhvānte rāja-yoghamajānatām |
haṭha-pradīpikāṃ dhatte svātmārāmaḥ kṛpākaraḥ || 3 |

Owing to the darkness arising from the multiplicity of opinions people are unable to know the Râja Yoga. Compassionate Swâtmârâma composes the Haṭha Yoga Pradipikâ like a torch to dispel it. 3.

हठ-विद्यां हि मत्स्येन्द्र-गोरक्श्हाद्या विजानते |
सवात्मारामो|अथवा योगी जानीते तत-परसादतः || ४ ||

haṭha-vidyāṃ hi matsyendra-ghorakṣhādyā vijānate |
svātmārāmo|athavā yoghī jānīte tat-prasādataḥ || 4 ||

Matsyendra, Gorakṣa, etc., knew Haṭha Vidyâ, and by their favour Yogî Swâtmârâma also learnt it from them. 4.

The following Siddhas (masters) are said to have existed in former times:—

शरी-आदिनाथ-मत्स्येन्द्र-शावरानन्द-भैरवाः |
छौरङ्गी-मीन-गोरक्श्ह-विरूपाक्श्ह-बिलेशयाः || ५ ||

śrī-ādinātha-matsyendra-śāvarānanda-bhairavāḥ |
chaurangghī-mīna-ghorakṣha-virūpākṣha-bileśayāḥ || 5 ||

Sri Âdinâtha (Śiva), Matsyendra, Nâtha, Sâbar, Anand, Bhairava, Chaurangi, Mîna nâtha, Gorakṣanâtha, Virupâkṣa, Bileśaya. 5.

मन्थानो भैरवो योगी सिद्धिर्बुद्धश्छ कन्थडिः |
कोरंटकः सुरानन्दः सिद्धपादश्छ छर्पटिः || ६ ||

manthāno bhairavo yoghī siddhirbuddhaścha kanthaḍiḥ |
koraṃṭakaḥ surānandaḥ siddhapādaścha charpaṭiḥ || 6 ||

Manthâna, Bhairava, Siddhi Buddha, Kanthadi, Karantaka, Surânanda, Siddhipâda, Charapati. 6.

कानेरी पूज्यपादश्छ नित्य-नाथो निरञ्जनः |
कपाली बिन्दुनाथश्छ काकछण्डीश्वराह्वयः || ७ ||

kānerī pūjyapādaścha nitya-nātho nirañjanaḥ |
kapālī bindunāthaścha kākachaṇḍīśvarāhvayaḥ || 7 ||

Kânerî, Pûjyapâda, Nityanâtha, Nirañjana, Kapâli, Vindunâtha, Kâka Chandîśwara. 7.

अल्लामः परभुदेवश्छ घोडा छोली छ टिंटिणिः |
भानुकी नारदेवश्छ खण्डः कापालिकस्तथा || ८ ||

allāmaḥ prabhudevaścha ghoḍā cholī cha ṭiṃṭiṇiḥ |
bhānukī nāradevaścha khaṇḍaḥ kāpālikastathā || 8 ||

Allâma, Prabhudeva, Ghodâ, Cholî, Tintiṇi, Bhânukî Nârdeva, Khanda Kâpâlika, etc. 8.

इत्यादयो महासिद्धा हठ-योग-परभावतः |
खण्डयित्वा काल-दण्डं बरह्माण्डे विछरन्ति ते || ९ ||

ityādayo mahāsiddhā haṭha-yogha-prabhāvataḥ |
khaṇḍayitvā kāla-daṇḍaṃ brahmāṇḍe vicharanti te || 9 ||

These Mahâsiddhas (great masters), breaking the sceptre of death, are roaming in the universe. 9.

अशेष्ह-ताप-तप्तानां समाश्रय-मठो हठः |
अशेष्ह-योग-युक्तानामाधार-कमठो हठः || १० ||

aśeṣha-tāpa-taptānāṃ samāśraya-maṭho haṭhaḥ |
aśeṣha-yogha-yuktānāmādhāra-kamaṭho haṭhaḥ || 10 ||

Like a house protecting one from the heat of the sun, Haṭha Yoga protects its practiser from the burning heat of the three Tâpas; and, similarly, it is the supporting tortoise, as it were, for those who are constantly devoted to the practice of Yoga. 10.

हठ-विद्या परं गोप्या योगिना सिद्धिमिछ्छता |
भवेद्वीर्यवती गुप्ता निर्वीर्या तु परकाशिता || ११ ||

haṭha-vidyā paraṃ ghopyā yoghinā siddhimichchatā | bhavedvīryavatī ghuptā nirvīryā tu prakāśitā || 11 ||

A Yogî desirous of success should keep the knowledge of Haṭha Yoga secret; for it becomes potent by concealing, and impotent by exposing. 11.

सुराज्ये धार्मिके देशे सुभिक्ष्हे निरुपद्रवे |
धनुः परमाण-पर्यन्तं शिलाग्नि-जल-वर्जिते |
एकान्ते मठिका-मध्ये सथातव्यं हठ-योगिना || १२ ||

surājye dhārmike deśe subhikṣhe nirupadrave | dhanuḥ pramāṇa-paryantaṃ śilāghni-jala-varjite | ekānte maṭhikā-madhye sthātavyaṃ haṭha-yoghinā || 12 ||

The Yogî should practise Haṭha Yoga in a small room, situated in a solitary place, being 4 cubits square, and free from stones, fire, water, disturbances of all kinds, and in a country where justice is properly administered, where good people live, and food can be obtained easily and plentifully. 12.

अल्प-दवारमरन्ध्र-गर्त-विवरं नात्युछ्छ-नीछायतं
सम्यग-गोमय-सान्द्र-लिप्तममलं निःशेस-जन्तूज्झितम |
बाह्ये मण्डप-वेदि-कूप-रुछिरं पराकार-संवेष्ह्टितं
परोक्तं योग-मठस्य लक्ष्हणमिदं सिद्धैर्हठाभ्यासिभिः || १३ ||

alpa-dvāramarandhra-gharta-vivaraṃ nātyuchcha-nīchāyataṃ samyagh-ghomaya-sāndra-liptamamalaṃ niḥśesa-jantūjjhitam | bāhye maṇḍapa-vedi-kūpa-ruchiraṃ prākāra-saṃveṣhṭitaṃ proktaṃ yogha-maṭhasya lakṣhaṇamidaṃ siddhairhaṭhābhyāsibhiḥ || 13 ||

The room should have a small door, be free from holes, hollows, neither too high nor too low, well plastered with cow-dung and free from dirt, filth and insects. On its outside there should be bowers, raised platform (chabootrâ), a well, and a compound. These characteristics of a room for Haṭha Yogîs have been described by adepts in the practice of Haṭha. 13.

एवं विधे मठे सथित्वा सर्व-छिन्ता-विवर्जितः |
गुरूपदिष्हट-मार्गेण योगमेव समभ्यसेत || १४ ||

evaṃ vidhe maṭhe sthitvā sarva-chintā-vivarjitaḥ |
ghurūpadiṣhṭa-mārgheṇa yoghameva samabhyaset || 14 ||

Having seated in such a room and free from all anxieties, he should practise Yoga, as instructed by his *guru*. 14.

अत्याहारः परयासश्छ परजल्पो नियमाग्रहः |
जन-सङ्गश्छ लौल्यं छ षहड्भिर्योगो विनश्यति || १५ ||

atyāhāraḥ prayāsaścha prajalpo niyamāghrahaḥ |
jana-sangghaścha laulyaṃ cha ṣhaḍbhiryogho vinaśyati || 15 ||

Yoga is destroyed by the following six causes:—Over-eating, exertion, talkativeness, adhering to rules, *i.e.*, cold bath in the morning, eating at night, or eating fruits only, company of men, and unsteadiness. 15.

उत्साहात्साहसाद्धैर्यात्तत्त्व-जञानाश्छ निश्छयात |
जन-सङ्ग-परित्यागात्ष्हड्भिर्योगः परसिद्ध्यति || १६ ||

utsāhātsāhasāddhairyāttattva-jñānāścha niśchayāt |
jana-sanggha-parityāghātṣhaḍbhiryoghaḥ prasiddhyati || 16 ||

The following six bring speedy success:—Courage, daring, perseverance, discriminative knowledge, faith, aloofness. from company. 16.

अथ यम-नियमाः
अहिंसा सत्यमस्तेयं बरह्मछर्यं कष्हमा धृतिः |
दयार्जवं मिताहारः शौछं छैव यमा दश || १७ ||

atha yama-niyamāḥ
ahiṃsā satyamasteyaṃ brahmacharyaṃ kṣhamā dhṛtiḥ |
dayārjavaṃ mitāhāraḥ śauchaṃ chaiva yamā daśa || 17 ||

The ten rules of conduct are: ahiṃsâ (non-injuring), truth, non-stealing, continence, forgiveness, endurance, compassion, meekness, sparing diet and cleanliness. 17.

तपः सन्तोष्ह आस्तिक्यं दानमीश्वर-पूजनम |
सिद्धान्त-वाक्य-शरवणं हरीमती छ तपो हुतम |
नियमा दश सम्प्रोक्ता योग-शास्त्र-विशारदैः || १८ ||

tapaḥ santoṣha āstikyaṃ dānamīśvara-pūjanam |
siddhānta-vākya-śravaṇaṃ hrīmatī cha tapo hutam |
niyamā daśa samproktā yogha-śāstra-viśāradaiḥ || 18 ||

The ten niyamas mentioned by those proficient in the knowledge of yoga are: Tapa, patience, belief in God, charity, adoration of God, hearing discourses on the principles of religion, shame, intellect, Tapa and Yajña. 18.

Âsanas.

अथ आसनम
हठस्य परथमाङ्गत्वादासनं पूर्वमुछ्यते |
कुर्यात्तदासनं सथैर्यमारोग्यं छाङ्ग-लाघवम || १९ ||

atha āsanam
haṭhasya prathamāngghatvādāsanaṃ pūrvamuchyate |
kuryāttadāsanaṃ sthairyamāroghyaṃ chāngghа-lāghavam || 19 ||

Being the first accessory of Haṭha Yoga, âsana is described first. It should be practised for gaining steady posture, health and lightness of body. 19.

वशिष्ह्ठाद्यैश्छ मुनिभिर्मत्स्येन्द्राद्यैश्छ योगिभिः |
अङ्गीकृतान्यासनानि कथ्यन्ते कानिछिन्मया || २० ||

vaśiṣhṭhādyaiścha munibhirmatsyendrādyaiścha yoghibhiḥ |
angghīkṛtānyāsanāni kathyante kānichinmayā || 20 ||

I am going to describe certain âsanas which have been adopted by Munîs like Vasiṣṭha, etc., and Yogîs like Matsyendra, etc. 20.

Swastika-âsana.

जानूर्वोरन्तरे सम्यक्कृत्वा पाद-तले उभे |
ऋजु-कायः समासीनः सवस्तिकं तत्प्रछक्ष्हते || २१ ||

jānūrvorantare samyakkṛtvā pāda-tale ubhe |
ṛju-kāyaḥ samāsīnaḥ svastikaṃ tatprachakṣhate || 21 ||

Having kept both the hands under both the thighs, with the body straight, when one sits calmly in this posture, it is called Swastika. 21.

Gomukha-âsana.

सव्ये दक्ष्हिण-गुल्कं तु पृष्ह्ठ-पार्श्वे नियोजयेत |
दक्ष्हिणे|अपि तथा सव्यं गोमुखं गोमुखाकृतिः || २२ ||

savye dakṣhiṇa-ghulkaṃ tu pṛṣhṭha-pārśve niyojayet |
dakṣhiṇe|api tathā savyaṃ ghomukhaṃ ghomukhākṛtiḥ || 22 ||

Placing the right ankle on the left side and the left ankle on the right side, makes Gomukha-âsana, having the appearance of a cow. 22.

Vîrâsana.

एकं पादं तथैकस्मिन्विन्यसेदुरुणि सथिरम |
इतरस्मिंस्तथा छोरुं वीरासनमितीरितम || २३ ||

ekaṃ pādaṃ tathaikasminvinyaseduruṇi sthiram |
itarasmiṃstathā choruṃ vīrāsanamitīritam || 23 ||

One foot is to be placed on the thigh of the opposite side; and so also the other foot on the opposite thigh. This is called Vîrâsana. 23.

Kurmâsana.

गुदं निरुध्य गुल्फाभ्यां वयुत्क्रमेण समाहितः |
कूर्मासनं भवेदेतदिति योग-विदो विदुः || २४ ||

ghudaṃ nirudhya ghulphābhyāṃ vyutkrameṇa samāhitaḥ |
kūrmāsanaṃ bhavedetaditi yogha-vido viduḥ || 24 ||

Placing the right ankle on the left side of anus, and the left ankle on the right side of it, makes what the Yogîs call Kûrma-âsana. 24.

Kukkuṭa âsana.

पद्मासनं तु संस्थाप्य जानूर्वोरन्तरे करौ । निवेश्य भूमौ संस्थाप्य वयोमस्थं कुक्कुटासनम || २५ ||

padmāsanaṃ tu saṃsthāpya jānūrvorantare karau | niveśya bhūmau saṃsthāpya vyomasthaṃ kukkuṭāsanam || 25 ||

Taking the posture of Padma-âsana and carrying the hands under the thighs, when the Yogî raises himself above the ground, with his palms resting on the ground, it becomes Kukkuṭa-âsana. 25.

Uttâna Kûrma-âsana.

कुक्कुटासन-बन्ध-सथो दोर्भ्यां सम्बद्य कन्धराम । भवेद्कूर्मवदुत्तान एतदुत्तान-कूर्मकम || २६ ||

kukkuṭāsana-bandha-stho dorbhyāṃ sambadya kandharām | bhavedkūrmavaduttāna etaduttāna-kūrmakam || 26 ||

Having assumed Kukkuṭa-âsana, when one grasps his neck by crossing his hands behind his head, and lies in this posture with his back touching the ground, it becomes Uttâna Kûrma-âsana, from its appearance like that of a tortoise. 26.

Dhanura âsana.

पादाङ्गुष्हठौ तु पाणिभ्यां गृहीत्वा शरवणावधि । धनुराकर्ष्हणं कुर्याद्धनुर-आसनमुछ्यते || २७ ||

pādāngghuṣhṭhau tu pāṇibhyāṃ ghṝhītvā śravaṇāvadhi | dhanurākarṣhaṇaṃ kuryāddhanur-āsanamuchyate || 27 ||

Having caught the toes of the feet with both the hands and carried them to the ears by drawing the body like a bow, it becomes Dhanura âsana. 27.

Matsya-âsana.

वामोरु-मूलार्पित-दक्ष्ह-पादं
जानोर्बहिर्वेष्ह्टित-वाम-पादम |
परगृह्य तिष्ह्ठेत्परिवर्तिताङ्गः
शरी-मत्य्सनाथोदितमासनं सयात || २८ ||
मत्स्येन्द्र-पीठं जठर-परदीप्तिं
परछण्ड-रुग्मण्डल-खण्डनास्त्रम |
अभ्यासतः कुण्डलिनी-परबोधं
छन्द्र-सथिरत्वं छ ददाति पुंसाम || २९ ||

vāmoru-mūlārpita-dakṣha-pādaṃ
jānorbahirveṣhṭita-vāma-pādam |
praghṝhya tiṣhṭhetparivartitāngghaḥ
śrī-matysanāthoditamāsanaṃ syāt || 28 ||
matsyendra-pīṭhaṃ jaṭhara-pradīptiṃ
prachaṇḍa-rughmaṇḍala-khaṇḍanāstram |
abhyāsataḥ kuṇḍalinī-prabodhaṃ
chandra-sthiratvaṃ cha dadāti puṃsām || 29 ||

Having placed the right foot at the root of the left thigh, let the toe be grasped with the right hand passing over the back, and having placed the left foot on the right thigh at its root, let it be grasped with the left hand passing behind the back. This is the âsana, as explained by Śri Matsyanâtha. It increases appetite and is an instrument for destroying the group of the most deadly diseases. Its practice awakens the Kundalinî, stops the nectar shedding from the moon in people. 28-29.

Paśchima Tâna.

परसार्य पादौ भुवि दण्ड-रूपौ
दोर्भ्यां पदाग्र-दवितयं गृहीत्वा |
जानूपरिन्यस्त-ललाट-देशो
वसेदिदं पश्छिमतानमाहुः || ३० ||

prasārya pādau bhuvi daṇḍa-rūpau
dorbhyāṃ padāghra-dvitayaṃ ghṝhītvā |
jānūparinyasta-lalāṭa-deśo
vasedidaṃ paśchimatānamāhuḥ || 30 ||

Having stretched the feet on the ground, like a stick, and having grasped the toes of both the feet with both the hands, when one sits with his forehead resting on the thighs, it is called Paśchima Tâna. 30.

इति पश्छिमतानमासनाग्र्यं
पवनं पश्छिम-वाहिनं करोति ।
उदयं जठरानलस्य कुर्याद
उदरे कार्श्यमरोगतां छ पुंसाम ॥ ३१ ॥

iti paśchimatānamāsanāghryaṃ
pavanaṃ paśchima-vāhinaṃ karoti |
udayaṃ jaṭharānalasya kuryād
udare kārśyamaroghatāṃ cha puṃsām || 31 ||

This Paśchima Tâna carries the air from the front to the back part of the body (*i.e.*, to the suṣumna). It kindles gastric fire, reduces obesity and cures all diseases of men. 31.

Mayûra-âsana.

धरामवष्ह्टभ्य कर-दवयेन
तत-कूर्पर-सथापित-नाभि-पार्श्वः ।
उछ्छासनो दण्डवदुत्थितः खे
मायूरमेतत्प्रवदन्ति पीठम ॥ ३२ ॥

dharāmavaṣhṭabhya kara-dvayena
tat-kūrpara-sthāpita-nābhi-pārśvaḥ |
uchchāsano daṇḍavadutthitaḥ khe
māyūrametatpravadanti pīṭham || 32 ||

Place the palms of both the hands on the ground, and place the navel on both the elbows and balancing thus, the body should be stretched backward like a stick. This is called Mayûra-âsana. 32.

हरति सकल-रोगानाशु गुल्मोदरादीन
अभिभवति छ दोष्हानासनं शरी-मयूरम ।
बहु कदशन-भुक्तं भस्म कुर्यादशेष्हं
जनयति जठराग्निं जारयेत्काल-कूटम ॥ ३३ ॥

harati sakala-roghānāśu ghulmodarādīn
abhibhavati cha doṣhānāsanaṃ śrī-mayūram |
bahu kadaśana-bhuktaṃ bhasma kuryādaśeṣhaṃ
janayati jaṭharāghniṃ jārayetkāla-kūṭam || 33 ||

This Âsana soon destroys all diseases, and removes abdominal disorders, and also those arising from irregularities of phlegm, bile and wind, digests unwholesome food taken in excess, increases appetite and destroys the most deadly poison. 33.

Śava-âsana.

उत्तानं शबवद्भूमौ शयनं तछ्छवासनम |
शवासनं शरान्ति-हरं छित्त-विश्रान्ति-कारकम || ३४ ||

uttānaṃ śabavadbhūmau śayanaṃ tachchavāsanam |
śavāsanaṃ śrānti-haraṃ chitta-viśrānti-kārakam || 34 ||

Lying down on the ground, like a corpse, is called Śava-âsana. It removes fatigue and gives rest to the mind. 34.

छतुरशीत्यासनानि शिवेन कथितानि छ |
तेभ्यश्छतुष्ह्कमादाय सारभूतं बरवीम्यहम || ३५ ||

chaturaśītyāsanāni śivena kathitāni cha |
tebhyaśchatuṣhkamādāya sārabhūtaṃ bravīmyaham || 35 ||

Śiva taught 84 âsanas. Of these the first four being essential ones, I am going to explain them here. 35.

सिद्धं पद्मं तथा सिंहं भद्रं वेति छतुष्हटयम |
शरेष्ह्ठं तत्रापि छ सुखे तिष्ह्ठेत्सिद्धासने सदा || ३६ ||

siddhaṃ padmaṃ tathā siṃhaṃ bhadraṃ veti chatuṣhṭayam |
śreṣhṭhaṃ tatrāpi cha sukhe tiṣhṭhetsiddhāsane sadā || 36 ||

These four are:—The Siddha, Padma, Sinha and Bhadra. Even of these, the Siddha-âsana, being very comfortable, one should always practise it. 36.

The Siddhâsana

अथ सिद्धासनम
योनि-सथानकमङ्घ्रि-मूल-घटितं कृत्वा दृढं विन्यसेत
मेण्ढ्रे पादमथैकमेव हृदये कृत्वा हनुं सुस्थिरम |
सथाणुः संयमितेन्द्रियो|अछल-दृशा पश्येद्भ्रुवोरन्तरं
हयेतन्मोक्ष्ह-कपाट-भेद-जनकं सिद्धासनं परोछ्यते || ३७ ||

atha siddhāsanam
yoni-sthānakamangghri-mūla-ghaṭitaṃ kṛtvā dṛḍhaṃ vinyaset meṇḍhre pādamathaikameva hṛdaye kṛtvā hanuṃ susthiram | sthāṇuḥ saṃyamitendriyo|achala-dṛśā paśyedbhruvorantaraṃ hyetanmokṣha-kapāṭa-bheda-janakaṃ siddhāsanaṃ prochyate || 37 ||

Press firmly the heel of the left foot against the perineum, and the right heel above the male organ. With the chin pressing on the chest, one should sit calmly, having restrained the senses, and gaze steadily the space between the eyebrows. This is called the Siddha Âsana, the opener of the door of salvation. 37.

मेण्ढ्रादुपरि विन्यस्य सव्यं गुल्फं तथोपरि | गुल्फान्तरं छ निक्षिहिप्य सिद्धासनमिदं भवेत || ३८ ||

meṇḍhrādupari vinyasya savyaṃ ghulphaṃ tathopari | ghulphāntaraṃ cha nikṣhipya siddhāsanamidaṃ bhavet || 38 ||

This Siddhâsana is performed also by placing the left heel on Meḍhra (above the male organ), and then placing the right one on it. 38.

एतत्सिद्धासनं प्राहुरन्ये वज्रासनं विदुः | मुक्तासनं वदन्त्येके प्राहुर्गुप्तासनं परे || ३९ ||

etatsiddhāsanaṃ prāhuranye vajrāsanaṃ viduḥ | muktāsanaṃ vadantyeke prāhurghuptāsanaṃ pare || 39 ||

Some call this Siddhâsana, some Vajrâsana. Others call it Mukta Âsana or Gupta Âsana. 39.

यमेष्ह्विव मिताहारमहिंसा नियमेष्ह्विव | मुख्यं सर्वासनेष्ह्वेकं सिद्धाः सिद्धासनं विदुः || ४० ||

yameṣhviva mitāhāramahiṃsā niyameṣhviva | mukhyaṃ sarvāsaneṣhvekaṃ siddhāḥ siddhāsanaṃ viduḥ || 40 ||

Just as sparing food is among Yamas, and Ahiṃsâ among the Niyamas, so is Siddhâsana called by adepts the chief of all the âsanas. 40.

छतुरशीति-पीठेष्हु सिद्धमेव सदाभ्यसेत | दवासप्तति-सहस्राणां नाडीनां मल-शोधनम || ४१ ||

chaturaśīti-pīṭheṣhu siddhameva sadābhyaset |
dvāsaptati-sahasrāṇāṃ nāḍīnāṃ mala-śodhanam || 41 ||

Out of the 84 Âsanas Siddhâsana should always be practised, because it cleanses the impurities of 72,000 nâḍîs. 41.

आत्म-धयायी मिताहारी यावद्द्वादश-वत्सरम |
सदा सिद्धासनाभ्यासाद्योगी निष्पत्तिमाप्नुयात || ४२ ||

ātma-dhyāyī mitāhārī yāvaddvādaśa-vatsaram |
sadā siddhāsanābhyāsādyoghī niṣhpattimāpnuyāt || 42 ||

By contemplating on oneself, by eating sparingly, and by practising Siddhâsana for 12 years, the Yogî obtains success. 42.

किमन्यैर्बहुभिः पीठैः सिद्धे सिद्धासने सति |
पराणानिले सावधाने बद्धे केवल-कुम्भके |
उत्पद्यते निरायासात्स्वयमेवोन्मनी कला || ४३ ||

kimanyairbahubhiḥ pīṭhaiḥ siddhe siddhāsane sati |
prāṇānile sāvadhāne baddhe kevala-kumbhake |
utpadyate nirāyāsātsvayamevonmanī kalā || 43 ||

Other postures are of no use, when success has been achieved in Siddhâsana, and Prâṇa Vâyû becomes calm and restrained by Kevala Kumbhaka. 43.

तथैकास्मिन्नेव दृढे सिद्धे सिद्धासने सति |
बन्ध-तरयमनायासात्स्वयमेवोपजायते || ४४ ||

tathaikāsminneva dṛḍhe siddhe siddhāsane sati |
bandha-trayamanāyāsātsvayamevopajāyate || 44 ||

Success in one Siddhâsana alone becoming firmly established, one gets Unmanî at once, and the three bonds (Bandhas) are accomplished of themselves. 44.

नासनं सिद्ध-सदृशं न कुम्भः केवलोपमः |
न खेछरी-समा मुद्रा न नाद-सदृशो लयः || ४५ ||

nāsanaṃ siddha-sadṛśaṃ na kumbhaḥ kevalopamaḥ |
na khecharī-samā mudrā na nāda-sadṛśo layaḥ || 45 ||

There is no Âsana like the Siddhâsana and no Kumbhaka like the Kevala. There is no mudrâ like the Khechari and no *laya* like the Nâda (Anâhata Nâda.) 45.

Padmâsana.

अथ पद्मासनम
वामोरूपरि दक्षिहिणं छ छरणं संस्थाप्य वामं तथा
दक्ष्होरूपरि पश्छिमेन विधिना धृत्वा कराभ्यां दृढम |
अङ्गुष्ह्ठौ हृदये निधाय छिबुकं नासाग्रमालोकयेत
एतद्व्याधि-विनाश-कारि यमिनां पद्मासनं परोछ्यते || ४६ ||

atha padmāsanam
vāmorūpari dakṣhiṇaṃ cha charaṇaṃ saṃsthāpya vāmaṃ tathā
dakṣhorūpari paśchimena vidhinā dhṛtvā karābhyāṃ dṛḍham |
angghuṣhṭhau hṛdaye nidhāya chibukaṃ nāsāghramālokayet
etadvyādhi-vināśa-kāri yamināṃ padmāsanaṃ prochyate || 46 ||

Place the right foot on the left thigh and the left foot on the right thigh, and grasp the toes with the hands crossed over the back. Press the chin against the chest and gaze on the tip of the nose. This is called the Padmâsana, the destroyer of the diseases of the Yamîs. 46.

उत्तानौ छरणौ कृत्वा ऊरु-संस्थौ परयत्नतः |
ऊरु-मध्ये तथोत्तानौ पाणी कृत्वा ततो दृशौ || ४७ ||

uttānau charaṇau kṛtvā ūru-saṃsthau prayatnataḥ |
ūru-madhye tathottānau pāṇī kṛtvā tato dṛśau || 47 ||

Place the feet on the thighs, with the soles upwards, and place the hands on the thighs, with the palms upwards. 47.

नासाग्रे विन्यसेद्राजद-अन्त-मूले तु जिह्वया |
उत्तम्भ्य छिबुकं वक्ष्हस्युत्थाप्य पवनं शनैः || ४८ ||

nāsāghre vinyasedrājad-anta-mūle tu jihvayā |
uttambhya chibukaṃ vakṣhasyutthāpy pavanaṃ śanaiḥ || 48 ||

Gaze on the tip of the nose, keeping the tongue pressed against the root of the teeth of the upper jaw, and the chin against the chest, and raise the air up slowly, *i.e.*, pull the apâna-vâyû gently upwards. 48.

इदं पद्मासनं परोक्तं सर्व-वयाधि-विनाशनम |
दुर्लभं येन केनापि धीमता लभ्यते भुवि || ४९ ||

idaṃ padmāsanaṃ proktaṃ sarva-vyādhi-vināśanam |
durlabhaṃ yena kenāpi dhīmatā labhyate bhuvi || 49 ||

This is called the Padmâsana, the destroyer of all diseases. It is difficult of attainment by everybody, but can be learnt by intelligent people in this world. 49.

कृत्वा सम्पुटितौ करौ दृढतरं बद्ध्वा तु पद्ममासनं
गाढं वक्ष्हसि सन्निधाय छिबुकं धयायंश्छ तच्छेतसि |
वारं वारमपानमूर्ध्वमनिलं परोत्सारयन्पूरितं
नयञ्छन्प्राणमुपैति बोधमतुलं शक्ति-परभावान्नरः || ५० ||

kṛtvā samputitau karau dṛḍhataraṃ baddhvā tu padmamāsanaṃ
ghāḍhaṃ vakṣhasi sannidhāya chibukaṃ dhyāyaṃścha tachchetasi |
vāraṃ vāramapānamūrdhvamanilaṃ protsārayanpūritaṃ
nyañchanprāṇamupaiti bodhamatulaṃ śakti-prabhāvānnaraḥ || 50 ||

Having kept both the hands together in the lap, performing the Padmâsana firmly, keeping the chin Fixed to the chest and contemplating on Him in the mind, by drawing the apâna-vâyû up (performing Mûla Bandha) and pushing down the air after inhaling it, joining thus the prâṇa and apâna in the navel, one gets the highest intelligence by awakening the śakti (kundalinî) thus. 50.

NB.—When Apâna Vâyû is drawn gently up and after filling in the lungs with the air from outside, the prâṇa is forced down by and by so as to join both of them in the navel, they both enter then the Kundalinî and, reaching the Brahma randhra (the great hole), they make the mind calm. Then the mind can contemplate on the nature of the âtmana and can enjoy the highest bliss.

पद्मासने सथितो योगी नाडी-दवारेण पूरितम |
मारुतं धारयेद्यस्तु स मुक्तो नात्र संशयः || ५१ ||

padmāsane sthito yoghī nāḍī-dvāreṇa pūritam |
mārutaṃ dhārayedyastu sa mukto nātra saṃśayaḥ || 51 ||

The Yogî who, sitting with Padmâsana, can control breathing, there is no doubt, is free from bondage. 51.

The Siṃhâsana.

अथ सिंहासनम
गुल्फौ छ वृष्हणस्याधः सीवन्त्याः पार्श्वयोः कष्हिपेत |
दक्षिहणे सव्य-गुल्फं तु दक्ष्ह-गुल्फं तु सव्यके || ५२ ||

atha simhāsanam
ghulphau cha vṝshaṇasyādhaḥ sīvantyāḥ pārśvayoḥ kṣhipet |
dakṣhiṇe savya-ghulphaṃ tu dakṣha-ghulphaṃ tu savyake || 52 ||

Press the heels on both sides of the seam of Perineum, in such a way that the left heel touches the right side and the right heel touches the left side of it. 52.

हस्तौ तु जान्वोः संस्थाप्य सवाङ्गुलीः सम्प्रसार्य छ |
वयात्त-वक्तो निरीक्ष्हेत नासाग्रं सुसमाहितः || ५३ ||

hastau tu jānvoḥ saṃsthāpya svāngghulīḥ samprasārya cha |
vyātta-vakto nirīkṣheta nāsāghraṃ susamāhitaḥ || 53 ||

Place the hands on the thighs, with stretched fingers, and keeping the mouth open and the mind collected, gaze on the tip of the nose. 53.

सिंहासनं भवेदेतत्पूजितं योगि-पुणगवैः |
बन्ध-तरितय-सन्धानं कुरुते छासनोत्तमम || ५४ ||

siṃhāsanaṃ bhavedetatpūjitaṃ yoghi-pungghavaiḥ |
bandha-tritaya-sandhānaṃ kurute chāsanottamam || 54 ||

This is Siṃhâsana, held sacred by the best of Yogîs. This excellent Âsana effects the completion of the three Bandhas (The Mûlabandha, Kanṭha or Jâlandhar Bandha and Uḍḍiyâna Bandha). 54.

The Bhadrâsana.

अथ भद्रासनम
गुल्फौ छ वृष्हणस्याधः सीवन्त्याः पार्श्वयोः कष्हिप्ते |
सव्य-गुल्फं तथा सव्ये दक्ष्ह-गुल्फं तु दक्षिहणे || ५५ ||
पार्श्व-पादौ छ पाणिभ्यां दृढं बद्ध्वा सुनिश्छलम |
भद्रासनं भवेदेतत्सर्व-वयाधि-विनाशनम |
गोरक्ष्हासनमित्याहुरिदं वै सिद्ध-योगिनः || ५६ ||

atha bhadrāsanam
ghulphau cha vṛṣhaṇasyādhaḥ sīvantyāḥ pārśvayoḥ kṣhipte |
savya-ghulphaṃ tathā savye dakṣha-ghulphaṃ tu dakṣhiṇe || 55 ||
pārśva-pādau cha pāṇibhyāṃ dṛḍhaṃ baddhvā suniśchalam |
bhadrāsanaṃ bhavedetatsarva-vyādhi-vināśanam |
ghorakṣhāsanamityāhuridaṃ vai siddha-yoghinaḥ || 56 ||

Place the heels on either side of the seam of the Perineum, keeping the left heel on the left side and the right one on the right side, hold the feet firmly joined to one another with both the hands. This Bhadrâsana is the destroyer of all the diseases. 55 and 56.

एवमासन-बन्धेष्हु योगीन्द्रो विगत-शरमः |
अभ्यसेन्नाडिका-शुद्धिं मुद्रादि-पवनी-करियाम || ५७ ||

evamāsana-bandheṣhu yoghīndro vighata-śramaḥ |
abhyasennāḍikā-śuddhiṃ mudrādi-pavanī-kriyām || 57 ||

The expert Yogîs call this Gorakśa âsana. By sitting with this âsana, the Yogî gets rid of fatigue 57.

आसनं कुम्भकं छित्रं मुद्राख्यं करणं तथा |
अथ नादानुसन्धानमभ्यासानुक्रमो हठे || ५८ ||

āsanaṃ kumbhakaṃ chitraṃ mudrākhyaṃ karaṇaṃ tathā |
atha nādānusandhānamabhyāsānukramo haṭhe || 58 ||

The Nâdis should be cleansed of their impurities by performing the mudrâs, etc., (which are the practices relating to the air) Âsanas, Kumbhakas and various curious mûdrâs. 58.

बरह्मछारी मिताहारी तयागी योग-परायणः |
अब्दादूर्ध्वं भवेद्सिद्धो नात्र कार्या विछारणा || ५९ ||

brahmachārī mitāhārī tyāghī yogha-parāyaṇaḥ |
abdādūrdhvaṃ bhavedsiddho nātra kāryā vichāraṇā || 59 ||

By regular and close attention to Nâda (anâhata nâda) in Haṭha Yoga, a Brahmachari, sparing in diet, unattached to objects of enjoyment, and devoted to Yoga, gains success, no doubt, within a year. 59.

सुस्निग्ध-मधुराहारश्छतुर्थांश-विवर्जितः |
भुज्यते शिव-सम्प्रीत्यै मिताहारः स उछ्यते || ६० ||

susnighdha-madhurāhāraśchaturthāṃśa-vivarjitaḥ |
bhujyate śiva-samprītyai mitāhāraḥ sa uchyate || 60 ||

Abstemious feeding is that in which ¾ of hunger is satisfied with food, well cooked with ghee and sweets, and eaten with the offering of it to Śiva. 60.

Foods injurious to a Yogî.

कट्वाम्ल-तीक्ष्हण-लवणोष्हण-हरीत-शाक-
सौवीर-तैल-तिल-सर्ष्हप-मद्य-मत्स्यान |
आजादि-मांस-दधि-तक्र-कुलत्थकोल-
पिण्याक-हिङ्गु-लशुनाद्यमपथ्यमाहुः || ६१ ||

kaṭvāmla-tīkṣhṇa-lavaṇoṣhṇa-harīta-śāka-
sauvīra-taila-tila-sarṣhapa-madya-matsyān |
ājādi-māṃsa-dadhi-takra-kulatthakola-
piṇyāka-hingghu-laśunādyamapathyamāhuḥ || 61 ||

Bitter, sour, saltish, hot, green vegetables, fermented, oily, mixed with til seed, rape seed, intoxicating liquors, fish, meat, curds, chhaasa pulses, plums, oil-cake, asafœtida (hînga), garlic, onion, etc., should not be eaten. 61.

भोजनमहितं विद्यात्पुनरस्योष्हणी-कृतं रूक्ष्हम |
अतिलवणमम्ल-युक्तं कदशन-शाकोत्कं वर्ज्यम || ६२ ||

bhojanamahitaṃ vidyātpunarasyoṣhṇī-kṛtaṃ rūkṣham |
atilavaṇamamla-yuktaṃ kadaśana-śākotkaṃ varjyam || 62 ||

Food heated again, dry, having too much salt, sour, minor grains, and vegetables that cause burning sensation, should not be eaten, Fire, women, travelling, etc., should be avoided. 62.

वह्नि-सत्री-पथि-सेवानामादौ वर्जनमाछरेत || ६३ ||

vahni-strī-pathi-sevānāmādau varjanamācharet || 63 ||

As said by Gorakṣa, one should keep aloof from the society of the evil-minded, fire, women, travelling, early morning bath, fasting, and all kinds of bodily exertion. 63.

तथा हि गोरक्ष्ह-वछनम
वर्जयेद्दुर्जन-परान्तं वहि्न-सत्री-पथि-सेवनम |
परातः-सनानोपवासादि काय-कलेश-विधिं तथा || ६४ ||

tathā hi ghorakṣha-vachanam
varjayeddurjana-prāntaṃ vahni-strī-pathi-sevanam |
prātaḥ-snānopavāsādi kāya-kleśa-vidhiṃ tathā || 64 ||

Wheat, rice, barley, shâstik (a kind of rice), good corns, milk, ghee, sugar, butter, sugarcandy, honey, dried ginger, Parwal (a vegetable) the five vegetables, moong, pure water, these are very beneficial to those who practise Yoga. 64.

गोधूम-शालि-यव-षहाष्ह्टिक-शोभनान्नं
कष्हीराज्य-खण्ड-नवनीत-सिद्धा-मधूनि |
शुण्ठी-पटोल-कफलादिक-पन्छ-शाकं
मुद्गादि-दिव्यमुदकं छ यमीन्द्र-पथ्यम || ६५ ||

ghodhūma-śāli-yava-ṣhāṣhṭika-śobhanānnaṃ
kṣhīrājya-khaṇḍa-navanīta-siddhā-madhūni |
śuṇṭhī-paṭola-kaphalādika-pañcha-śākaṃ
mudghādi-divyamudakaṃ cha yamīndra-pathyam || 65 ||

A Yogî should eat tonics (things giving strength), well sweetened, greasy (made with ghee), milk, butter, etc., which may increase humors of the body, according to his desire. 65.

पुष्ह्टं सुमधुरं सनिग्धं गव्यं धातु-परपोष्हणम |
मनोभिलष्हितं योग्यं योगी भोजनमाछरेत || ६६ ||

puṣhṭaṃ sumadhuraṃ snighdhaṃ ghavyaṃ dhātu-prapoṣhaṇam |
manobhilaṣhitaṃ yoghyaṃ yoghī bhojanamācharet || 66 ||

Whether young, old or too old, sick or lean, one who discards laziness, gets success if he practises Yoga. 66.

युवो वृद्धो|अतिवृद्धो वा वयाधितो दुर्बलो|अपि वा |
अभ्यासात्सिद्धिमाप्नोति सर्व-योगेष्ह्वतन्द्रितः || ६७ ||

yuvo vṝddho|ativṝddho vā vyādhito durbalo|api vā |
abhyāsātsiddhimāpnoti sarva-yogheṣhvatandritaḥ || 67 ||

Success comes to him who is engaged in the practice. How can one get success without practice; for by merely reading books on Yoga, one can never get success. 67.

करिया-युक्तस्य सिद्धिः सयादक्रियस्य कथं भवेत |
न शास्त्र-पाठ-मात्रेण योग-सिद्धिः परजायते || ६८ ||

kriyā-yuktasya siddhiḥ syādakriyasya kathaṃ bhavet |
na śāstra-pāṭha-mātreṇa yogha-siddhiḥ prajāyate || 68 ||

Success cannot be attained by adopting a particular dress (Veṣa). It cannot be gained by telling tales. Practice alone is the means to success. This is true, there is no doubt. 68.

न वेष्ह-धारणं सिद्धेः कारणं न छ तत-कथा |
करियैव कारणं सिद्धेः सत्यमेतन्न संशयः || ६९ ||
पीठानि कुम्भकाश्छित्रा दिव्यानि करणानि छ |
सर्वाण्यपि हठाभ्यासे राज-योग-फलावधि || ७० ||

na veṣha-dhāraṇaṃ siddheḥ kāraṇaṃ na cha tat-kathā |
kriyaiva kāraṇaṃ siddheḥ satyametanna saṃśayaḥ || 69 ||
pīṭhāni kumbhakāśchitrā divyāni karaṇāni cha |
sarvāṇyapi haṭhābhyāse rāja-yogha-phalāvadhi || 70 ||

Âsanas (postures), various Kumbhakas, and other divine means, all should be practised in the practice of Haṭha Yoga, till the fruit—Râja Yoga—is obtained. 69.

End of chapter 1st, on the method of forming the Âsanas.

इति हठ-परदीपिकायां परथमोपदेशः |

iti haṭha-pradīpikāyāṃ prathamopadeśaḥ |

CHAPTER II.

On Prâṇâyâma.

|| २ || दवितीयोपदेशः

|| 2 || dvitīyopadeśaḥ

अथासने दृधे योगी वशी हित-मिताशनः | गुरूपदिष्ह्ट-मार्गेण पराणायामान्समभ्यसेत || १ ||

athāsane dṝdhe yoghī vaśī hita-mitāśanaḥ | ghurūpadiṣhṭa-mārgheṇa prāṇāyāmānsamabhyaset || 1 ||

Posture becoming established, a Yogî, master of himself, eating salutary and moderate food, should practise Prâṇâyâma, as instructed by his guru. 1.

छले वाते छलं छित्तं निश्छले निश्छलं भवेत|| योगी सथाणुत्वमाप्नोति ततो वायुं निरोधयेत || २ ||

chale vāte chalaṃ chittaṃ niśchale niśchalaṃ bhavet|| yoghī sthāṇutvamāpnoti tato vāyuṃ nirodhayet || 2 ||

Respiration being disturbed, the mind becomes disturbed. By restraining respiration, the Yogî gets steadiness of mind 2.

यावद्वायुः सथितो देहे तावज्जीवनमुछ्यते | मरणं तस्य निष्ह्क्रान्तिस्ततो वायुं निरोधयेत || ३ ||

yāvadvāyuḥ sthito dehe tāvajjīvanamuchyate | maraṇaṃ tasya niṣhkrāntistato vāyuṃ nirodhayet || 3 ||

So long as the (breathing) air stays in the body, it is called life. Death consists in the passing out of the (breathing) air. It is, therefore, necessary to restrain the breath. 3.

मलाकलासु नाडीष्हु मारुतो नैव मध्यगः |
कथं सयादुन्मनीभावः कार्य-सिद्धिः कथं भवेत || ४ ||

malākalāsu nāḍīṣhu māruto naiva madhyaghaḥ |
kathaṃ syādunmanībhāvaḥ kārya-siddhiḥ kathaṃ bhavet || 4 ||

The breath does not pass through the middle channel (suṣumnâ), owing to the impurities of the nâdîs. How can then success be attained, and how can there be the unmanî avasthâ. 4.

शुद्धमेति यदा सर्वं नाडी-छक्रं मलाकुलम |
तदैव जायते योगी पराण-संग्रहणे कष्हमः || ५ ||

śuddhameti yadā sarvaṃ nāḍī-chakraṃ malākulam |
tadaiva jāyate yoghī prāṇa-saṃghrahaṇe kṣhamaḥ || 5 ||

When the whole system of nâdîs which is full of impurities, is cleaned, then the Yogî becomes able to control the Prâṇa. 5.

पराणायामं ततः कुर्यान्नित्यं सात्त्विकया धिया |
यथा सुष्हुम्णा-नाडीस्था मलाः शुद्धिं परयान्ति छ || ६ ||

prāṇāyāmaṃ tataḥ kuryānnityaṃ sāttvikayā dhiyā |
yathā suṣhumṇā-nāḍīsthā malāḥ śuddhiṃ prayānti cha || 6 ||

Therefore, Prâṇâyâma should be performed daily with sâtwika buddhi (intellect free from raja and tama or activity and sloth), in order to drive out the impurities of the suṣumnâ. 6.

Method of performing Prâṇâyâma.

बद्ध-पद्मासनो योगी पराणं छन्द्रेण पूरयेत |
धारयित्वा यथा-शक्ति भूयः सूर्येण रेछयेत || ७ ||
पराणं सूर्येण छाकृष्ह्य पूरयेदुदरं शनैः |
विधिवत्कुम्भकं कृत्वा पुनश्छन्द्रेण रेछयेत || ८ ||

baddha-padmāsano yoghī prāṇaṃ chandreṇa pūrayet |
dhārayitvā yathā-śakti bhūyaḥ sūryeṇa rechayet || 7 ||
prāṇaṃ sūryeṇa chākṛṣhya pūrayedudaraṃ śanaiḥ |
vidhivatkumbhakaṃ kṛtvā punaśchandreṇa rechayet || 8 ||

Sitting in the Padmâsana posture the Yogî should fill in the air through the left nostril (closing the right one); and, keeping it confined according to one's ability, it should be expelled slowly through the sûrya (right nostril). Then, drawing in the air through the sûrya (right nostril) slowly, the belly should be filled, and after performing Kumbhaka as before, it should be expelled slowly through the chandra (left nostril). 7 and 8.

येन तयजेत्तेन पीत्वा धारयेदतिरोधतः |
रेछयेछछ ततो|अन्येन शनैरेव न वेगतः || ९ ||

yena tyajettena pītvā dhārayedatirodhataḥ |
rechayechcha tato|anyena śanaireva na veghataḥ || 9 ||

Inhaling thus through the one, through which it was expelled, and having restrained it there, till possible, it should be exhaled through the other, slowly and not forcibly. 9.

पराणं छेदिडया पिबेन्नियमितं भूयो|अन्यथा रेछयेत
पीत्वा पिङ्गलया समीरणमथो बद्ध्वा तयजेद्वामया |
सूर्य-छन्द्रमसोरनेन विधिनाभ्यासं सदा तन्वतां
शुद्धा नाडि-गणा भवन्ति यमिनां मास-तरयादूर्ध्वतः || १० ||

prāṇaṃ chediḍayā pibenniyamitaṃ bhūyo|anyathā rechayet
pītvā pingghalayā samīraṇamatho baddhvā tyajedvāmayā |
sūrya-chandramasoranena vidhinābhyāsaṃ sadā tanvatāṃ
śuddhā nāḍi-ghaṇā bhavanti yamināṃ māsa-trayādūrdhvataḥ || 10 ||

If the air be inhaled through the left nostril, it should be expelled again through the other, and filling it through the right nostril, confining it there, it should be expelled through the left nostril. By practising in this way, through the right and the left nostrils alternately, the whole of the collection of the nâdîs of the yamîs (practisers) becomes clean, *i.e.*, free from impurities, after 3 months and over. 10.

परातर्मध्यन्दिने सायमर्ध-रात्रे छ कुम्भकान |
शनैरशीति-पर्यन्तं छतुर्वारं समभ्यसेत || ११ ||

prātarmadhyandine sāyamardha-rātre cha kumbhakān |
śanairaśīti-paryantaṃ chaturvāraṃ samabhyaset || 11 ||

Kumbhakas should be performed gradually 4 times during day and night, *i.e.*, (morning, noon, evening and midnight), till the number of Kumbhakas for one time is 80 and for day and night together it is 320. 11.

कनीयसि भवेद्स्वेद कम्पो भवति मध्यमे ।
उत्तमे सथानमाप्नोति ततो वायुं निबन्धयेत ॥ १२ ॥

kanīyasi bhavedsveda kampo bhavati madhyame |
uttame sthānamāpnoti tato vāyuṃ nibandhayet || 12 ||

In the beginning there is perspiration, in the middle stage there is quivering, and in the last or the 3rd stage one obtains steadiness; and then the breath should be made steady or motionless. 12.

जलेन शरम-जातेन गात्र-मर्दनमाछरेत ।
दृढता लघुता छैव तेन गात्रस्य जायते ॥ १३ ॥

jalena śrama-jātena ghātra-mardanamācharet |
dṝḍhatā laghutā chaiva tena ghātrasya jāyate || 13 ||

The perspiration exuding from exertion of practice should be rubbed into the body (and not wiped), as by so doing the body becomes strong. 13.

अभ्यास-काले परथमे शस्तं कष्हीराज्य-भोजनम ।
ततो।अभ्यासे दृढीभूते न तादृङ-नियम-गरहः ॥ १४ ॥

abhyāsa-kāle prathame śastaṃ kṣhīrājya-bhojanam |
tato|abhyāse dṝḍhībhūte na tādṝng-niyama-ghrahaḥ || 14 ||

During the first stage of practice the food consisting of milk and ghee is wholesome. When the practice becomes established, no such restriction is necessary. 14.

यथा सिंहो गजो वयाघ्रो भवेद्वश्यः शनैः शनैः ।
तथैव सेवितो वायुरन्यथा हन्ति साधकम ॥ १५ ॥

yathā siṃho ghajo vyāghro bhavedvaśyaḥ śanaiḥ śanaiḥ |
tathaiva sevito vāyuranyathā hanti sādhakam || 15 ||

Just as lions, elephants and tigers are controlled by and by, so the breath is controlled by slow degrees, otherwise (*i.e.*, by being hasty or using too much force) it kills the practiser himself. 15.

पराणायामेन युक्तेन सर्व-रोग-कष्हयो भवेत |
अयुक्ताभ्यास-योगेन सर्व-रोग-समुद्गमः || १६ ||

prāṇāyāmena yuktena sarva-rogha-kṣhayo bhavet |
ayuktābhyāsa-yoghena sarva-rogha-samudghamaḥ || 16 ||

When Prâṇayama, etc., are performed properly, they eradicate all diseases; but an improper practice generates diseases. 16.

हिक्का शवासश्छ कासश्छ शिरः-कर्णाक्ष्हि-वेदनाः |
भवन्ति विविधाः रोगाः पवनस्य परकोपतः || १७ ||

hikkā śvāsaścha kāsaścha śiraḥ-karṇākṣhi-vedanāḥ |
bhavanti vividhāḥ roghāḥ pavanasya prakopataḥ || 17 ||

Hiccough, asthma, cough, pain in the head, the ears, and the eyes; these and other various kinds of diseases are generated by the disturbance of the breath. 17.

युक्तं युक्तं तयजेद्वायुं युक्तं युक्तं छ पूरयेत |
युक्तं युक्तं छ बध्नीयादेवं सिद्धिमवाप्नुयात || १८ ||

yuktaṃ yuktaṃ tyajedvāyuṃ yuktaṃ yuktaṃ cha pūrayet |
yuktaṃ yuktaṃ cha badhnīyādevaṃ siddhimavāpnuyāt || 18 ||

The air should be expelled with proper tact and should be filled in skilfully; and when it has been kept confined properly it brings success. 18.

NB.—The above caution is necessary to warn the aspirants against omitting any instruction; and, in their zeal to gain success or siddhis early, to begin the practice, either by using too much force in filling in, confining and expelling the air, or by omitting any instructions, it may cause unnecessary pressure on their ears, eyes, &c„ and cause pain. Every word in the instructions is full of meaning and is necessarily used in the slokas, and should be followed very carefully and with due attention. Thus there will be nothing to fear whatsoever. We are inhaling and exhaling the air throughout our lives without any sort of danger, and Prâṇayama being only a regular form of it, there should be no cause to fear.

यदा तु नाडी-शुद्धिः सयात्तथा छिह्नानि बाह्यतः |
कायस्य कृशता कान्तिस्तदा जायते निश्छितम || १९ ||

yadā tu nāḍī-śuddhiḥ syāttathā chihnāni bāhyataḥ | kāyasya kṛśatā kāntistadā jāyate niśchitam || 19 ||

When the nâdîs become free from impurities, and there appear the outward signs of success, such as lean body and glowing colour, then one should feel certain of success. 19.

यथेष्ह्टं धारणं वायोरनलस्य परदीपनम |
नादाभिव्यक्तिरारोग्यं जायते नाडि-शोधनात || २० ||

yatheṣhṭaṃ dhāraṇaṃ vāyoranalasya pradīpanam | nādābhivyaktirāroghyaṃ jāyate nāḍi-śodhanāt || 20 ||

By removing the impurities, the air can be restrained, according to one's wish and the appetite is increased, the divine sound is awakened, and the body becomes healthy. 20.

मेद-शलेष्ह्माधिकः पूर्वं षहट-कर्माणि समाछरेत |
अन्यस्तु नाछरेत्तानि दोष्हाणां समभावतः || २१ ||

meda-śleṣhmādhikaḥ pūrvaṃ ṣhaṭ-karmāṇi samācharet | anyastu nācharettāni doṣhāṇāṃ samabhāvataḥ || 21 ||

If there be excess of fat or phlegm in the body, the six kinds of kriyâs (duties) should be performed first. But others, not suffering from the excess of these, should not perform them. 21.

धौतिर्बस्तिस्तथा नेतिस्त्राटकं नौलिकं तथा |
कपाल-भातिश्छैतानि षहट-कर्माणि परछक्ष्हते || २२ ||

dhautirbastistathā netistrāṭakaṃ naulikaṃ tathā | kapāla-bhātiśchaitāni ṣhaṭ-karmāṇi prachakṣhate || 22 ||

The six kinds of duties are: Dhauti, Basti, Neti, Trâtaka, Nauti and Kapâla Bhâti. These are called the six actions वट्कमि 22.

कर्म षहट्कमिदं गोप्यं घट-शोधन-कारकम |
विछित्र-गुण-सन्धाय पूज्यते योगि-पुणगवैः || २३ ||

karma ṣhaṭkamidaṃ ghopyaṃ ghaṭa-śodhana-kārakam | vichitra-ghuṇa-sandhāya pūjyate yoghi-pungghavaiḥ || 23 ||

These six kinds of actions which cleanse the body should be kept secret. They produce extraordinary attributes and are performed with earnestness by the best of Yogîs. 23.

The Dhauti (धौति)

तत्र धौतिः
छतुर-अङ्गुल-विस्तारं हस्त-पञ्छ-दशायतम |
गुरूपदिष्हट-मार्गेण सिक्तं वस्त्रं शनैर्ग्रसेत |
पुनः परत्याहरेच्छैतदुदितं धौति-कर्म तत || २४ ||

tatra dhautiḥ
chatur-angghula-vistāraṃ hasta-pañcha-daśāyatam |
ghurūpadiṣhṭa-mārgheṇa siktaṃ vastraṃ śanairghraset |
punaḥ pratyāharechchaitaduditaṃ dhauti-karma tat || 24 ||

A strip of cloth, about 3 inches wide and 15 cubits long, is pushed in (swallowed), when moist with warm water, through the passage shown by the guru, and is taken out again. This is called Dhauti Karma. 24.

NB.—The strip should be moistened with a little warm water, and the end should be held with the teeth. It is swallowed slowly, little by little; thus, first day 1 cubit, 2nd day 2 cubits, 3rd day 3 cubits, and so on. After swallowing it the stomach should be given a good, round motion from left to right, and then it should be taken out slowly and gently.

कास-शवास-पलीह-कुष्हठं कफरोगाश्छ विंशतिः |
धौति-कर्म-परभावेण परयान्त्येव न संशयः || २५ ||

kāsa-śvāsa-plīha-kuṣhṭhaṃ kapharoghāścha viṃśatiḥ |
dhauti-karma-prabhāveṇa prayāntyeva na saṃśayaḥ || 25 ||

There is no doubt, that cough, asthma, enlargement of the spleen, leprosy, and 20 kinds of diseases born of phlegm, disappear by the practice of Dhauti Karma. 25.

The Basti (बस्तिकर्म)

अथ बस्तिः
नाभि-दघ्न-जले पायौ नयस्त-नालोत्कटासनः |
आधाराकुनछनं कुर्यात्क्ष्हालनं बस्ति-कर्म तत || २६ ||

atha bastiḥ
nābhi-daghna-jale pāyau nyasta-nālotkaṭāsanaḥ |
ādhārākuñchanaṃ kuryātkṣhālanaṃ basti-karma tat || 26 ||

Squatting in navel-deep water, and introducing a six inches long, smooth piece of ½ an inch diameter pipe, open at both ends, half inside the anus; it (anus) should he drawn up (contracted) and then expelled. This washing is called the Basti Karma. 26.

गुल्म-पलीहोदरं छापि वात-पित्त-कफोद्भवाः |
बस्ति-कर्म-परभावेण कष्हीयन्ते सकलामयाः || २७ ||

ghulma-plīhodaraṃ chāpi vāta-pitta-kaphodbhavāḥ |
basti-karma-prabhāveṇa kṣhīyante sakalāmayāḥ || 27 ||

By practising this Basti Karma, colic, enlarged spleen, and dropsy, arising from the disorders of Vâta (air), pitta (bile) and kapha (phlegm), are all cured. 27.

धान्त्वद्रियान्तः-करण-परसादं
दधाछ्छ कान्तिं दहन-परदीप्तम |
अशेष्ह-दोष्होपछयं निहन्याद
अभ्यस्यमानं जल-बस्ति-कर्म || २८ ||

dhāntvadriyāntaḥ-karaṇa-prasādaṃ
dadhāchcha kāntiṃ dahana-pradīptam |
aśeṣha-doṣhopachayaṃ nihanyād
abhyasyamānaṃ jala-basti-karma || 28 ||

By practising Basti with water, the Dhâtâs, the Indriyas and the mind become calm. It gives glow and tone to the body and increases the appetite. All the disorders disappear. 28.

The Neti (नेति).

अथ नेतिः
सूत्रं वितस्ति-सुस्निग्धं नासानाले परवेशयेत |
मुखान्निर्गमयेछ्छैष्हा नेतिः सिद्धैर्निगद्यते || २९ ||

atha netiḥ
sūtraṃ vitasti-susnighdhaṃ nāsānāle praveśayet |
mukhānnirghamayechchaiṣhā netiḥ siddhairnighadyate || 29 ||

A cord made of threads and about six inches long, should be passed through the passage of the nose and the end taken out in the mouth. This is called by adepts the Neti Karma. 29.

कपाल-शोधिनी छैव दिव्य-दृष्ट्टि-परदायिनी ।
जत्रूर्ध्व-जात-रोगौघं नेतिराशु निहन्ति छ ॥ ३० ॥

kapāla-śodhinī chaiva divya-dṝṣhṭi-pradāyinī ।
jatrūrdhva-jāta-roghaughaṃ netirāśu nihanti cha ॥ 30 ॥

The Neti is the cleaner of the brain and giver of divine sight. It soon destroys all the diseases of the cervical and scapular regions. 30.

The Trâtaka (तराटक).

अथ तराटकम
निरीक्षहेन्निश्छल-दृशा सूक्ष्हम-लक्ष्हयं समाहितः ।
अश्रु-सम्पात-पर्यन्तमाछार्यैस्त्राटकं समृतम ॥ ३१ ॥

atha trāṭakam
nirīkṣhenniśchala-dṝśā sūkṣhma-lakṣhyaṃ samāhitaḥ ।
aśru-sampāta-paryantamāchāryaistrāṭakaṃ smṝtam ॥ 31 ॥

Being calm, one should gaze steadily at a small mark, till eyes are filled with tears. This is called Trataka by âchâryas. 31.

मोछनं नेत्र-रोगाणां तन्दाद्रीणां कपाटकम ।
यत्नतस्त्राटकं गोप्यं यथा हाटक-पेटकम ॥ ३२ ॥

mochanaṃ netra-roghāṇāṃ tandādrīṇāṃ kapāṭakam ।
yatnatastrāṭakaṃ ghopyaṃ yathā hāṭaka-peṭakam ॥ 32 ॥

Trâtaka destroys the eye diseases and removes sloth, etc. It should be kept secret very carefully, like a box of jewellery. 32.

The Nauli (नौलि).

अथ नौलिः
अमन्दावर्त-वेगेन तुन्दं सव्यापसव्यतः ।
नतांसो भरामयेदेष्हा नौलिः सिद्धैः परशस्यते ॥ ३३ ॥

atha nauliḥ
amandāvarta-veghena tundaṃ savyāpasavyataḥ |
natāṃso bhrāmayedeṣhā nauliḥ siddhaiḥ praśasyate || 33 ||

Sitting on the toes with heels raised above the ground, and the palms resting on the ground, and in this bent posture the belly is moved forcibly from left to right just, as in vomiting. This is called by adepts the Nauli Karma. 33.

मन्दाग्नि-सन्दीपन-पाछ्नादि-
सन्धापिकानन्द-करी सदैव |
अशेष्ह-दोष्ह-मय-शोष्हणी छ
हठ-करिया मौलिरियं छ नौलिः || ३४ ||

mandāghni-sandīpana-pāchanādi-
sandhāpikānanda-karī sadaiva |
aśeṣha-doṣha-maya-śoṣhaṇī cha
haṭha-kriyā mauliriyaṃ cha nauliḥ || 34 ||

It removes dyspepsia, increases appetite and digestion, and is like the goddess of creation, and causes happiness. It dries up all the disorders. This Nauli is an excellent exercise in Haṭha Yoga. 34.

The Kapâla Bhâti कपाल भाति.

अथ कपालभातिः
भस्त्रावल्लोह-कारस्य रेछ-पूरौ ससम्भ्रमौ |
कपालभातिर्विख्याता कफ-दोष्ह-विशोष्हणी || ३५ ||

atha kapālabhātiḥ
bhastrāvalloha-kārasya recha-pūrau sasambhramau |
kapālabhātirvikhyātā kapha-doṣha-viśoṣhaṇī || 35 ||

When inhalation and exhalation are performed very quickly, like a pair of bellows of a blacksmith, it dries up all the disorders from the excess of phlegm, and is known as Kapâla Bhâti. 35.

षहट-कर्म-निर्गत-सथौल्य-कफ-दोष्ह-मलादिकः |
पराणायामं ततः कुर्यादनायासेन सिद्ध्यति || ३६ ||

ṣhaṭ-karma-nirghata-sthaulya-kapha-doṣha-malādikaḥ |
prāṇāyāmaṃ tataḥ kuryādanāyāsena siddhyati || 36 ||

When Prâṇâyâma is performed after getting rid of obesity born of the defects phlegm, by the performance of the six duties, it easily brings success 36.

पराणायामैरेव सर्वे परशुष्हयन्ति मला इति |
आछार्याणां तु केष्हांछिदन्यत्कर्म न संमतम || ३७ ||

prāṇāyāmaireva sarve praśuṣhyanti malā iti |
āchāryāṇāṃ tu keṣhāṃchidanyatkarma na saṃmatam || 37 ||

Some âchâryâs (teachers) do not advocate any other practice, being of opinion that all the impurities are dried up by the practice of Prâṇâyâma. 37.

Gaja Karaṇi (गजकरणी)

अथ गज-करणी
उदर-गत-पदार्थमुद्वमन्ति
पवनमपानमुदीर्य कण्ठ-नाले |
करम-परिछय-वश्य-नाडि-छक्रा
गज-करणीति निगद्यते हठज्ञैः || ३८ ||

atha ghaja-karaṇī
udara-ghata-padārthamudvamanti
pavanamapānamudīrya kaṇṭha-nāle |
krama-parichaya-vaśya-nāḍi-chakrā
ghaja-karaṇīti nighadyate haṭhajñaiḥ || 38 ||

By carrying the Apâna Vâyû up to the throat, the food, etc., in the stomach are vomited. By degrees, the system of Nâdîs (Śankhinî) becomes known. This is called in Haṭha as Gaja Karaṇi. 38.

बरह्मादयो|अपि तरिदशाः पवनाभ्यास-तत्पराः |
अभूवन्नन्तक-भयात्तस्मात्पवनमभ्यसेत || ३९ ||

brahmādayo|api tridaśāḥ pavanābhyāsa-tatparāḥ |
abhūvannantaka-bhyāttasmātpavanamabhyaset || 39 ||

Brahmâ, and other Devas were always engaged in the exercise of Prâṇâyâma, and, by means of it, got rid of the fear of death. Therefore, one should practise prâṇâyâma regularly. 39.

यावद्बद्धो मरुद-देशे यावच्छित्तं निराकुलम |
यावद्दृष्टिर्भ्रुवोर्मध्ये तावत्काल-भयं कुतः || ४० ||

yāvadbaddho marud-deśe yāvachchittaṃ nirākulam |
yāvaddṛṣhṭirbhruvormadhye tāvatkāla-bhayaṃ kutaḥ || 40 ||

So long as the breath is restrained in the body, so long as the mind is undisturbed, and so long as the gaze is fixed between the eyebrows, there is no fear from Death. 40.

विधिवत्प्राण-संयामैर्नाडी-छक्रे विशोधिते |
सुष्हुम्णा-वदनं भित्त्वा सुखाद्विशति मारुतः || ४१ ||

vidhivatprāṇa-saṃyāmairnāḍī-chakre viśodhite |
suṣhumṇā-vadanaṃ bhittvā sukhādviśati mārutaḥ || 41 ||

When the system of Nâdis becomes clear of the impurities by properly controlling the prâṇa, then the air, piercing the entrance of the Suśumṇâ, enters it easily. 41.

Manomanî. (मनोन्मनी)

अथ मनोन्मनी
मारुते मध्य-संछारे मनः-सथैर्यं परजायते |
यो मनः-सुस्थिरी-भावः सैवावस्था मनोन्मनी || ४२ ||

atha manonmanī
mārute madhya-saṃchāre manaḥ-sthairyaṃ prajāyate |
yo manaḥ-susthirī-bhāvaḥ saivāvasthā manonmanī || 42 ||

Steadiness of mind comes when the air moves Freely in the middle. That is the manonmanî (मनोन्मनी) condition, which is attained when the mind becomes calm. 42.

तत-सिद्धये विधानज्ञाश्छित्रान्कुर्वन्ति कुम्भकान |
विछित्र कुम्भकाभ्यासाद्विछित्रां सिद्धिमाप्नुयात || ४३ ||

tat-siddhaye vidhānajñāśchitrānkurvanti kumbhakān |
vichitra kumbhakābhyāsādvichitrāṃ siddhimāpnuyāt || 43 ||

To accomplish it, various Kumbhakas are performed by those who are expert in the methods; for, by the practice of different Kumbhakas, wonderful success is attained. 43

Different hinds of Kumbhakas.

अथ कुम्भक-भेदाः
सूर्य-भेदनमुज्जायी सीत्कारी शीतली तथा ।
भस्त्रिका भरामरी मूछर्छा पलाविनीत्यष्हट-कुम्भकाः || ४४ ||

atha kumbhaka-bhedāḥ
sūrya-bhedanamujjāyī sītkārī śītalī tathā |
bhastrikā bhrāmarī mūrchchā plāvinītyaṣhṭa-kumbhakāḥ || 44 ||

Kumbhakas are of eight kinds, viz., Sûrya Bhedan, Ujjâyî, Sîtkarî, Sîtalî, Bhastrikâ, Bhrâmarî, Mûrchhâ, and Plâvinî. 44

पूरकान्ते तु कर्तव्यो बन्धो जालन्धराभिधः ।
कुम्भकान्ते रेछकादौ कर्तव्यस्तूड्डियानकः || ४५ ||

pūrakānte tu kartavyo bandho jālandharābhidhaḥ |
kumbhakānte rechakādau kartavyastūḍḍiyānakaḥ || 45 ||

At the end of Pûraka, Jâlandhara Bandha should be performed, and at the end of Kumbhaka, and at the beginning of Rechaka, Uddiyâna Bandha should be performed. 45

NḄ.—Pûraka is filling in of the air from outside.

Kumbhaka is the keeping the air confined inside. Rechaka is expelling the confined air. The instructions for Puraka, Kumbhaka and Rechaka will be found at their proper place and should he carefully followed.

अधस्तात्कुनछ्नेनाशु कण्ठ-सङ्कोछने कृते ।
मध्ये पश्छिम-तानेन सयात्प्राणो बरह्म-नाडिगः || ४६ ||

adhastātkuñchanenāśu kaṇṭha-sangkochane kṛte |
madhye paśchima-tānena syātprāṇo brahma-nāḍighaḥ || 46 ||

By drawing up from below (Mûla Bandha) and contracting the throat (Jâlandhara Bandha) and by pulling back the middle of the front portion of the body (*i.e.*, belly), the Prâṇa goes to the Brahma Nâdî (Suṣumnâ). 46

The middle hole, through the vertebral column, through which the spinal cord passes, is called the Suṣumnâ Nâdî of the Yogîs. The two other sympathetic cords, one on each aide of the spinal cord, are called the Idâ and the Pingalâ Nâdîs. These will be described later on.

आपानमूर्ध्वमुत्थाप्य पराणं कण्ठादधो नयेत |
योगी जरा-विमुक्तः सन्ष्होडशाब्द-वया भवेत || ४७ ||

āpānamūrdhvamutthāpya prāṇaṃ kaṇṭhādadho nayet |
yoghī jarā-vimuktaḥ sanṣhoḍaśābda-vayā bhavet || 47 ||

By pulling up the Apâna Vâyu and by forcing the Prâṇa Vâyu down the throat, the Yogî, liberated from old age, becomes young, as it were 16 years old. 47

Note.—

हृदि प्राणो गुदेऽपानः समानो नाभिमण्डले ।
उदानः कण्ठदेशस्थो व्यानः सर्वशरीरगः । शिवसंहितायाम् प्र० ३ श्लो० ७ ।

The seat of the Prâṇa is the heart; of the Apâna anus; of the Samâna the region about the navel; of the Udâna the throat; while the Vyâna moves throughout the body.

Sûrya Bhedana (सूर्य भेदन).

अथ सूर्य-भेदनम
आसने सुखदे योगी बद्ध्वा छैवासनं ततः |
दक्ष्ह-नाड्या समाकृष्ह्य बहिःस्थं पवनं शनैः || ४८ ||

atha sūrya-bhedanam
āsane sukhade yoghī baddhvā chaivāsanaṃ tataḥ |
dakṣha-nāḍyā samākṛṣhya bahiḥsthaṃ pavanaṃ śanaiḥ || 48 ||

Taking any comfortable posture and performing the âsana, the Yogî should draw in the air slowly, through the right nostril. 48

आकेशादानखाग्राच्छ निरोधावधि कुम्भयेत |
ततः शनैः सव्य-नाड्या रेछयेत्पवनं शनैः || ४९ ||

ākeśādānakhāghrāchcha nirodhāvadhi kumbhayet |
tataḥ śanaiḥ savya-nāḍyā rechayetpavanaṃ śanaiḥ || 49 ||

Then it should be confined within, so that it fills from the nails to the tips of the hair, and then let out through the left nostril slowly. 49

Note.—This is to be done alternately with both the nostrils, drawing in through the one, expelling through the other, and vice versa.

कपाल-शोधनं वात-दोष्ह-घ्नं कृमि-दोष्ह-हृत |
पुनः पुनरिदं कार्यं सूर्य-भेदनमुत्तमम || ५० ||

kapāla-śodhanaṃ vāta-doṣha-ghnaṃ kṝmi-doṣha-hṝt |
punaḥ punaridaṃ kāryaṃ sūrya-bhedanamuttamam || 50 ||

This excellent Sûrya Bhedana cleanses the forehead (frontal sinuses), destroys the disorders of Vâta, and removes the worms, and, therefore, it should be performed again and again. 50

Translation: I am going to describe the procedure of the practice of Yoga, in order that Yogîs may succeed. A wise man should leave his bed in the Uṣâ Kâla (*i.e.*, at the peep of dawn or 4 o'clock) in the morning. 1.

Remembering his guru over his head, and his desired deity in his heart, after answering the calls of nature, and cleaning his mouth, he should apply Bhaṣma (ashes). 2.

In a clean spot, clean room and charming ground, he should spread a soft âsana (cloth for sitting on). Having seated on it and remembering, in his mind his guru and his God. 3.

Having extolled the place and the time and taking up the vow thus: 'To day by the grace of God, I will perform Prâṇâyâmas with âsanas for gaining samâdhi (trance) and its fruits.' He should salute the infinite Deva, Lord of the Nâgas, to ensure success in the âsanas (postures). 4.

Salutation to the Lord of the Nâgas, who is adorned with thousands of heads, set with brilliant jewels (maṇis), and who has sustained the whole universe, nourishes it, and is infinite. After this he should begin his exercise of âsanas and when fatigued, he should practise Śava âsana. Should there be no fatigue, he should not practise it. 5.

Before Kumbhaka, he should perform Viparîta Karṇî mudrâ, in order that he may be able to perform Jâlandhar bandha comfortably. 6.

Sipping a little water, he should begin the exercise of Prâṇâyâma, after saluting Yogindras, as described in the Karma Parana, in the words of Śiva. 7.

Such as "Saluting Yogindras and their disciples and gurû Vinâyaka, the Yogî should unite with me with composed mind." 8.

While practising, he should sit with Siddhâsana, and having performed *bandha* and Kumbhaka, should begin with 10 Prâṇâyâmas the first day, and go on increasing 5 daily. 9.

With composed mind 80 Kumbhakas should be performed at a time; beginning first with the chandra (the left nostril) and then sûrya (the right nostril). 10.

This has been spoken of by wise men as Aṇuloma and Viloma. Having practised Sûrya Bhedan, with Bandhas, the wise rust) should practise Ujjâyî and then Sîtkârî Śîtalî, and Bhastrikâ, he may practice others or not. 11-12.

He should practise mudrâs properly, as instructed by his guru. Then sitting with Padmâsana, he should hear anâhata nâda attentively. 13.

He should *resign the fruits of all his practice reverently to God*, and, on rising on the completion of the practice, a warm bath should be taken. 14.

The bath should bring all the daily duties briefly to an end. At noon also a little rest should be taken at the end of the exercise, and then food should be taken. 15.

Yogîs should always take wholesome food and never anything unwholesome. After dinner he should eat Ilâchî or lavanga. 16.

Some like camphor, and betel leaf. To the Yogîs, practising Prâṇâyâma, betel leaf without powders, i, e., lime, nuts and kâtha, is beneficial. 17.

After taking food he should read books treating of salvation, or hear Purâṇas and repeat the name of God. 18.

In the evening the exercise should be begun after finishing sandyhâ, as before, beginning the practice 3 ghatikâ or one hour before the sun sets. 19.

Evening sandhyâ should always be performed after practice, and Haṭha Yoga should be practised at midnight. 20.

Viparîta Karṇi is to be practised in the evening and at midnight, and not just after eating, as it does no good at this time. 21.

Ujjâyî (उज्जायी)

अथ उज्जायी
मुखं संयम्य नाडीभ्यामाकृष्ह्य पवनं शनैः ।
यथा लगति कण्ठात्तु हृदयावधि स-सवनम || ५१ ||

atha ujjāyī
mukhaṃ saṃyamya nāḍībhyāmākṛṣhya pavanaṃ śanaiḥ |
yathā laghati kaṇṭhāttu hṛdayāvadhi sa-svanam || 51 ||

Having closed the opening of the Nâdî (Larynx), the air should be drawn in such a way that it goes touching from the throat to the chest, and making noise while passing. 51.

पूर्ववत्कुम्भयेत्प्राणं रेछयेदिडया तथा ।
शलेष्हम-दोष्ह-हरं कण्ठे देहानल-विवर्धनम || ५२ ||

pūrvavatkumbhayetprāṇaṃ rechayediḍayā tathā |
śleṣhma-doṣha-haraṃ kaṇṭhe dehānala-vivardhanam || 52 ||

It should be restrained, as before, and then let out through Idâ (the left nostril). This removes śleṣmâ (phlegm) in the throat and increases the appetite. 52.

नाडी-जलोदराधातु-गत-दोष्ह-विनाशनम ।
गछ्छता तिष्ह्ठता कार्यमुज्जाय्याख्यं तु कुम्भकम || ५३ ||

nāḍī-jalodarādhātu-ghata-doṣha-vināśanam |
ghachchatā tiṣhṭhatā kāryamujjāyyākhyaṃ tu kumbhakam || 53 ||

It destroys the defects of the nâdîs, dropsy and disorders of Dhâtu (humours). Ujjâyî should be performed in all conditions of life, even while walking or sitting. 53.

Sîtkârî (सीत्कारी)

अथ सीत्कारी
सीत्कां कुर्यात्तथा वक्त्रे घराणेनैव विजृम्भिकाम ।
एवमभ्यास-योगेन काम-देवो दवितीयकः || ५४ ||

atha sītkārī
sītkāṃ kuryāttathā vaktre ghrāṇenaiva vijṝmbhikām |
evamabhyāsa-yoghena kāma-devo dvitīyakaḥ || 54 ||

Sîtkârî is performed by drawing in the air through the mouth, keeping the tongue between the lips. The air thus drawn in should not be expelled through the mouth. By practising in this way, one becomes next to the God of Love in beauty. 54.

योगिनी छक्र-संमान्यः सृष्हिट-संहार-कारकः ।
न कष्हुधा न तृष्हा निद्रा नैवालस्यं परजायते || ५५ ||

yoghinī chakra-saṃmānyaḥ sṛṣhṭi-saṃhāra-kārakaḥ |
na kṣhudhā na tṛṣhā nidrā naivālasyaṃ prajāyate || 55 ||

He is regarded adorable by the Yoginîs and becomes the destroyer of the cycle of creation, He is not afflicted with hunger, thirst, sleep or lassitude. 55.

भवेत्सत्त्वं छ देहस्य सर्वोपद्रव-वर्जितः |
अनेन विधिना सत्यं योगीन्द्रो भूमि-मण्डले || ५६ ||

bhavetsattvaṃ cha dehasya sarvopadrava-varjitaḥ |
anena vidhinā satyaṃ yoghīndro bhūmi-maṇḍale || 56 ||

The Satwa of his body becomes free from all the disturbances. In truth, he becomes the lord of the Yogîs in this world. 56.

Śîtalî (शीतली)

अश शीतली
जिह्वया वायुमाकृष्ह्य पूर्ववत्कुम्भ-साधनम |
शनकैर्घ्राण-रन्ध्राभ्यां रेछयेत्पवनं सुधीः || ५७ ||

atha śītalī
jihvayā vāyumākṛṣhya pūrvavatkumbha-sādhanam |
śanakairghrāṇa-randhrābhyāṃ rechayetpavanaṃ sudhīḥ || 57 ||

As in the above (Sîtkári), the tongue to be protruded a little out of the lips, when the air is drawn in. It is kept confined, as before, and then expelled slowly through the nostrils. 57.

गुल्म-पलीहादिकान्रोगान्ज्वरं पित्तं कष्हुधां तृष्हाम |
विष्हाणि शीतली नाम कुम्भिकेयं निहन्ति हि || ५८ ||

ghulma-plīhādikānroghānjvaraṃ pittaṃ kṣhudhāṃ tṛṣhām |
viṣhāṇi śītalī nāma kumbhikeyaṃ nihanti hi || 58 ||

This Śîtalî Ḳumbhikâ cures colic, (enlarged) spleen, fever, disorders of bile, hunger, thirst, and counteracts poisons. 58.

The Bhastrikâ (भस्त्रिका)

अथ भस्त्रिका

ऊर्वोरुपरि संस्थाप्य शुभे पाद-तले उभे |
पद्मासनं भवेदेतत्सर्व-पाप-परणाशनम || ५९ ||

atha bhastrikā
ūrvorupari saṃsthāpya śubhe pāda-tale ubhe |
padmāsanaṃ bhavedetatsarva-pāpa-praṇāśanam || 59 ||

The Padma Âsana consists in crossing the feet and placing them on both the thighs; it is the destroyer of all sins. 59.

सम्यक्पद्मासनं बद्ध्वा सम-गरीवोदरः सुधीः |
मुखं संयम्य यत्नेन पराणं घराणेन रेछयेत || ६० ||

samyakpadmāsanaṃ baddhvā sama-ghrīvodaraḥ sudhīḥ |
mukhaṃ saṃyamya yatnena prāṇaṃ ghrāṇena rechayet || 60 ||

Binding the Padma-Âsana and keeping the body straight, closing the mouth carefully, let the air be expelled through the nose. 60.

यथा लगति हृत-कण्ठे कपालावधि स-सवनम |
वेगेन पूरयेछ्छापि हृत-पद्मावधि मारुतम || ६१ ||

yathā laghati hṝt-kaṇṭhe kapālāvadhi sa-svanam |
veghena pūrayechchāpi hṝt-padmāvadhi mārutam || 61 ||

It should be filled up to the lotus of the heart, by drawing it in with force, making noise and touching the throat, the chest and the head. 61.

पुनर्विरेछयेत्तद्वत्पूरयेछ्छ पुनः पुनः |
यथैव लोहकारेण भस्त्रा वेगेन छाल्यते || ६२ ||

punarvirechayettadvatpūrayechcha punaḥ punaḥ |
yathaiva lohakāreṇa bhastrā veghena chālyate || 62 ||

It should he expelled again and filled again and again as before, just as a pair of bellows of the blacksmith is worked. 62.

तथैव सव-शरीर-सथं छालयेत्पवनं धिया |
यदा शरमो भवेद्देहे तदा सूर्येण पूरयेत || ६३ ||

tathaiva sva-śarīra-sthaṃ chālayetpavanaṃ dhiyā |
yadā śramo bhaveddehe tadā sūryeṇa pūrayet || 63 ||

In the same way, the air of the body should be moved intelligently, filling it through Sûrya when fatigue is experienced. 63.

यथोदरं भवेत्पूर्णमनिलेन तथा लघु |
धारयेन्नासिकां मध्या-तर्जनीभ्यां विना दृढम || ६४ ||

yathodaraṃ bhavetpūrṇamanilena tathā laghu |
dhārayennāsikāṃ madhyā-tarjanībhyāṃ vinā dṛḍham || 64 ||

The air should be drawn in through the right nostril by pressing the thumb against the left side of the nose, so as to close the left nostril; and when filled to the full, it should be closed with the fourth finger (the one next to the little finger) and kept confined. 64.

विधिवत्कुम्भकं कृत्वा रेछयेदिडयानिलम |
वात-पित्त-शलेष्हम-हरं शरीराग्नि-विवर्धनम || ६५ ||

vidhivatkumbhakaṃ kṛtvā rechayediḍayānilam |
vāta-pitta-śleṣhma-haraṃ śarīrāghni-vivardhanam || 65 ||

Having confined it properly, it should be expelled through the Idâ (left nostril). This destroys Vâta, pitta (bile) and phlegm and increases the digestive power (the gastric fire). 65.

कुण्डली बोधकं कष्हिप्रं पवनं सुखदं हितम |
बरह्म-नाडी-मुखे संस्थ-कफाद्य-अर्गल-नाशनम || ६६ ||

kuṇḍalī bodhakaṃ kṣhipraṃ pavanaṃ sukhadaṃ hitam |
brahma-nāḍī-mukhe saṃstha-kaphādy-arghala-nāśanam || 66 ||

It quickly awakens the Kuṇḍalinî, purifies the system, gives pleasure, and is beneficial. It destroys phlegm and the impurities accumulated at the entrance of the Brahma Nâdî. 66.

सम्यग्गात्र-समुद्भूत-गरन्थि-तरय-विभेदकम |
विशेष्हेणैव कर्तव्यं भस्त्राख्यं कुम्भकं तविदम || ६७ ||

samyaghghātra-samudbhūta-ghranthi-traya-vibhedakam |
viśeṣheṇaiva kartavyaṃ bhastrākhyaṃ kumbhakaṃ tvidam || 67 ||

This Bhastrikâ should be performed plentifully, for it breaks the three knots: Brahma granthi (in the chest), Viṣṇu granthi (in the throat), and Rudra granthi (between the eyebrows) of the body. 67.

The Bhrâmari (भरामरी)

अथ भरामरी
वेगाद्घोष्हं पूरकं भृङ्ग-नादं
भृङ्गी-नादं रेछकं मन्द-मन्दम |
योगीन्द्राणमेवमभ्यास-योगाछ
छित्ते जाता काछिदानन्द-लीला || ६८ ||

atha bhrāmarī
veghādghoṣhaṃ pūrakaṃ bhṝnggha-nādaṃ
bhṝngghī-nādaṃ rechakaṃ manda-mandam |
yoghīndrāṇamevamabhyāsa-yoghāch
chitte jātā kāchidānanda-līlā || 68 ||

By filling the air with force, making noise like Bhringi (wasp), and expelling it slowly, making noise in the same way; this practice causes a sort of ecstacy in the minds of Yogîndras. 68.

The Mûrchhâ (मूर्छा).

अथ मूछर्छा
पूरकान्ते गाढतरं बद्ध्वा जालन्धरं शनैः |
रेछयेन्मूछर्छाख्येयं मनो-मूछर्छा सुख-परदा || ६९ ||

atha mūrchchā
pūrakānte ghāḍhataraṃ baddhvā jālandharaṃ śanaiḥ |
rechayenmūrchchākhyeyaṃ mano-mūrchchā sukha-pradā || 69 ||

Closing the passages with Jâlandhar Bandha firmly at the end of Pûraka, and expelling the air slowly, is called Mûrchhâ, from its causing the mind to swoon and giving comfort. 69.

The Plâvinî (पलाविनी).

अथ पलाविनी
अन्तः परवर्तितोदार-मारुतापूरितोदरः |
पयस्यगाधे|अपि सुखात्प्लवते पद्म-पत्रवत || ७० ||

atha plāvinī antaḥ pravartitodāra-mārutāpūritodaraḥ | payasyaghādhe|api sukhātplavate padma-patravat || 70 ||

When the belly is filled with air and the inside of the body is filled to its utmost with air, the body floats on the deepest water, like the leaf of a lotus. 70.

पराणायामस्त्रिधा परोक्तो रेछ-पूरक-कुम्भकैः | सहितः केवलश्छेति कुम्भको दविविधो मतः || ७१ ||

prāṇāyāmastridhā prokto recha-pūraka-kumbhakaiḥ | sahitaḥ kevalaścheti kumbhako dvividho mataḥ || 71 ||

Considering Pûraka (Filling), Rechaka (expelling) and Kumbhaka (confining), Prâṇâyâma is of three kinds, but considering it accompanied by Pûraka and Rechaka, and without these, it is of two kinds only, *i.e.*, Sahita (with) and Kevala (alone). 71.

यावत्केवल-सिद्धिः सयात्सहितं तावदभ्यसेत | रेछकं पूरकं मुक्त्वा सुखं यद्वायु-धारणम || ७२ ||

yāvatkevala-siddhiḥ syātsahitaṃ tāvadabhyaset | rechakaṃ pūrakaṃ muktvā sukhaṃ yadvāyu-dhāraṇam || 72 ||

Exercise in Sahita should be continued till success in Kevala is gained. This latter is simply confining the air with ease, without Rechaka and Pûraka. 72.

पराणायामो|अयमित्युक्तः स वै केवल-कुम्भकः | कुम्भके केवले सिद्धे रेछ-पूरक-वर्जिते || ७३ ||

prāṇāyāmo|ayamityuktaḥ sa vai kevala-kumbhakaḥ | kumbhake kevale siddhe recha-pūraka-varjite || 73 ||

In the practice of Kevala Prâṇâyâma when it can be performed successfully without Rechaka and Pûraka, then it is called Kevala Kumbhaka. 73.

न तस्य दुर्लभं किंछित्त्रिष्हु लोकेष्हु विद्यते | शक्तः केवल-कुम्भेन यथेष्हटं वायु-धारणात || ७४ ||

na tasya durlabhaṃ kiṃchittriṣhu lokeṣhu vidyate | śaktaḥ kevala-kumbhena yatheṣhṭaṃ vāyu-dhāraṇāt || 74 ||

There is nothing in the three worlds which may be difficult to obtain for him who is able to keep the air confined according to pleasure, by means of Kevala Kumbhaka. 74.

राज-योग-पदं छापि लभते नात्र संशयः ।
कुम्भकात्कुण्डली-बोधः कुण्डली-बोधतो भवेत ।
अनर्गला सुष्हुम्णा छ हठ-सिद्धिश्छ जायते ॥ ७५ ॥

rāja-yogha-padaṃ chāpi labhate nātra saṃśayaḥ |
kumbhakātkuṇḍalī-bodhaḥ kuṇḍalī-bodhato bhavet |
anarghalā suṣhumṇā cha haṭha-siddhiścha jāyate || 75 ||

He obtains the position of Râja Yoga undoubtedly. Kuṇḍalinî awakens by Kumbhaka, and by its awakening, Suṣumnâ becomes free from impurities. 75.

हठं विना राजयोगो राज-योगं विना हठः ।
न सिध्यति ततो युग्ममानिष्हपत्तेः समभ्यसेत ॥ ७६ ॥

haṭhaṃ vinā rājayogho rāja-yoghaṃ vinā haṭhaḥ |
na sidhyati tato yughmamāniṣhpatteḥ samabhyaset || 76 ||

No success in Râja Yoga without Haṭha Yoga, and no success in Haṭha Yoga without Râja Yoga. One should, therefore, practise both of these well, till complete success is gained. 76.

कुम्भक-पराण-रोधान्ते कुर्याछ्छित्तं निराश्रयम ।
एवमभ्यास-योगेन राज-योग-पदं वरजेत ॥ ७७ ॥

kumbhaka-prāṇa-rodhānte kuryāchchittaṃ nirāśrayam |
evamabhyāsa-yoghena rāja-yogha-padaṃ vrajet || 77 ||

On the completion of Kumbhaka, the mind should be given rest. By practising in this way one is raised to the position of (succeeds in getting) Râja Yoga. 77.

Indications of success in the practice of Haṭha Yoga.

वपुः कृशत्वं वदने परसन्नता
नाद-सफुटत्वं नयने सुनिर्मले ।
अरोगता बिन्दु-जयो।अग्नि-दीपनं
नाडी-विशुद्धिर्हठ-सिद्धि-लक्ष्हणम ॥ ७८ ॥

vapuḥ kṝśatvaṃ vadane prasannatā nāda-sphuṭatvaṃ nayane sunirmale | aroghatā bindu-jayo|aghni-dīpanaṃ nāḍī-viśuddhirhaṭha-siddhi-lakṣhaṇam || 78 ||

When the body becomes lean, the face glows with delight, Anâhatanâda manifests, and eyes are clear, body is healthy, *bindu* under control, and appetite increases, then one should know that the Nâdîs are purified and success in Haṭha Yoga is approaching. 78.

End of Chapter II.

इति हठ-परदीपिकायां दवितीयोपदेशः |

iti haṭha-pradīpikāyāṃ dvitīyopadeśaḥ |

CHAPTER III.

On Mudrâs.

|| ३ || तृतीयोपदेशः

|| 3 || tṛtīyopadeśaḥ

स-शैल-वन-धात्रीणां यथाधारो|अहि-नायकः |
सर्वेष्हां योग-तन्त्राणां तथाधारो हि कुण्डली || १ ||

sa-śaila-vana-dhātrīṇāṃ yathādhāro|ahi-nāyakaḥ |
sarveṣhāṃ yogha-tantrāṇāṃ tathādhāro hi kuṇḍalī || 1 ||

As the chief of the snakes is the support of the earth with all the mountains and forests on it, so all the Tantras (Yoga practices) rest on the Kuṇḍalinî. (The Vertebral column.) 1.

सुप्ता गुरु-परसादेन यदा जागर्ति कुण्डली |
तदा सर्वाणि पद्मानि भिद्यन्ते गरन्थयो|अपि छ || २ ||

suptā ghuru-prasādena yadā jāgharti kuṇḍalī |
tadā sarvāṇi padmāni bhidyante ghranthayo|api cha || 2 ||

When the sleeping Kuṇḍalinî awakens by favour of a guru, then all the lotuses (in the six chakras or centres) and all the knots are pierced through. 2.

पराणस्य शून्य-पदवी तदा राजपथायते |
तदा छित्तं निरालम्बं तदा कालस्य वञ्छनम || ३ ||

prāṇasya śūnya-padavī tadā rājapathāyate |
tadā chittaṃ nirālambaṃ tadā kālasya vañchanam || 3 ||

Suṣumnâ (Sûnya Padavî) becomes a main road for the passage of Prâṇa, and the mind then becomes free from all connections (with its objects of enjoyments) and Death is then evaded. 3.

सुष्हुम्णा शून्य-पदवी बरह्म-रन्ध्रः महापथः । शमशानं शाम्भवी मध्य-मार्गश्छेत्येक-वाछकाः || ४ ||

suṣhumṇā śūnya-padavī brahma-randhraḥ mahāpathaḥ | śmaśānaṃ śāmbhavī madhya-mārghaśchetyeka-vāchakāḥ || 4 ||

Suṣumnâ, Sunya Padavî, Brahma Randhra, Mahâ Patha, Śmaśâna, Śambhavî, Madhya Mârga, are names of one and the same thing. 4.

तस्मात्सर्व-परयत्नेन परबोधयितुमीश्वरीम । बरह्म-दवार-मुखे सुप्तां मुद्राभ्यासं समाछरेत || ५ ||

tasmātsarva-prayatnena prabodhayitumīśvarīm | brahma-dvāra-mukhe suptāṃ mudrābhyāsaṃ samācharet || 5 ||

In order, therefore, to awaken this goddess, who is sleeping at the entrance of Brahma Dwâra (the great door), mudrâs should be practised well. 5.

The mudrâs.

महामुद्रा महाबन्धो महावेधश्छ खेछरी । उड्डीयानं मूलबन्धश्छ बन्धो जालन्धराभिधः || ६ ||

mahāmudrā mahābandho mahāvedhaścha khecharī | uḍḍīyānaṃ mūlabandhaścha bandho jālandharābhidhaḥ || 6 ||

Mahâ Mudrâ, Mahâ Bandha, Mahâ Vedha, Khecharî, Uḍḍiyâna Bandha, Mûla Bandha, Jâlandhara Bandha. 6.

करणी विपरीताख्या वज्रोली शक्ति-छालनम । इदं हि मुद्रा-दशकं जरा-मरण-नाशनम || ७ ||

karaṇī viparītākhyā vajrolī śakti-chālanam | idaṃ hi mudrā-daśakaṃ jarā-maraṇa-nāśanam || 7 ||

Viparîta Karaṇî, Vajroli, and Śakti Châlana. These are the ten Mudrâs which annihilate old age and death. 7.

आदिनाथोदितं दिव्यमष्हटैश्वर्य-परदायकम । वल्लभं सर्व-सिद्धानां दुर्लभं मरुतामपि || ८ ||

ādināthoditaṃ divyamaṣhṭaiśvarya-pradāyakam |
vallabhaṃ sarva-siddhānāṃ durlabhaṃ marutāmapi || 8 ||

They have been explained by Âdi Nâtha (Śiva) and give eight kinds of divine wealth. They are loved by all the Siddhas and are hard to attain even by the Marutas. 8.

Note.—The eight *Aiśwaryas* are: Aṇimâ (becoming small, like an atom), Mahimâ (becoming great, like âkâs, by drawing in atoms of Prakṛiti), Garimâ (light things, like cotton becoming very heavy like mountains.)

Prâpti (coming within easy reach of everything; as touching the moon with the little finger, while standing on the earth.)

Prâkâmya (non-resistance to the desires, as entering the earth like water.)

Îsatâ (mastery over matter and objects made of it.)

Vaśitwa (controlling the animate and inanimate objects.)

गोपनीयं परयत्नेन यथा रत्न-करण्डकम |
कस्यचिन्नैव वक्तव्यं कुल-सत्री-सुरतं यथा || ९ ||

ghopanīyaṃ prayatnena yathā ratna-karaṇḍakam |
kasyachinnaiva vaktavyaṃ kula-strī-surataṃ yathā || 9 ||

These Mudrâs should be kept secret by every means, as one keeps one's box of jewellery, and should, on no account be told to any one, just as husband and wife keep their dealings secret. 9.

The mahâ mudrâ.

अथ महा-मुद्रा
पाद-मूलेन वामेन योनिं सम्पीड्य दक्ष्हिणाम |
परसारितं पदं कृत्वा कराभ्यां धारयेद्दृढम || १० ||

atha mahā-mudrā
pāda-mūlena vāmena yoniṃ sampīḍya dakṣhiṇām |
prasāritaṃ padaṃ kṛtvā karābhyāṃ dhārayeddṛḍham || 10 ||

Pressing the Yoni (perineum) with the heel of the left foot, and stretching forth the right foot, its toe should be grasped by the thumb and first finger. 10.

कण्ठे बन्धं समारोप्य धारयेद्वायुमूर्ध्वतः |
यथा दण्ड-हतः सर्पो दण्डाकारः परजायते || ११ ||

ऋज्वीभूता तथा शक्तिः कुण्डली सहसा भवेत |
तदा सा मरणावस्था जायते दविपुटाश्रया || १२ ||

kaṇṭhe bandhaṃ samāropya dhārayedvāyumūrdhvataḥ |
yathā daṇḍa-hataḥ sarpo daṇḍākāraḥ prajāyate || 11 ||
ṛjvībhūtā tathā śaktiḥ kuṇḍalī sahasā bhavet |
tadā sā maraṇāvasthā jāyate dvipuṭāśrayā || 12 ||

By stopping the throat (by Jâlandhara Bandha) the air is drawn in from the outside and carried down. Just as a snake struck with a stick becomes straight like a stick, in the same way, *śakti* (suṣumnâ) becomes straight at once. Then the Kuṇḍalinî, becoming as it were dead, and, leaving both the Idâ and the Pingalâ, enters the suṣumnâ (the middle passage). 11-12.

ततः शनैः शनैरेव रेछयेन्नैव वेगतः |
महा-मुद्रां छ तेनैव वदन्ति विबुधोत्तमाः || १३ ||

tataḥ śanaiḥ śanaireva rechayennaiva veghataḥ |
mahā-mudrāṃ cha tenaiva vadanti vibudhottamāḥ || 13 ||

It should be expelled then, slowly only and not violently. For this very reason, the best of the wise men call it the Mahâ Mudrâ. This Mahâ Mudrâ has been propounded by great masters. 13.

इयं खलु महामुद्रा महा-सिद्धैः परदर्शिता |
महा-कलेशादयो दोष्हाः कष्हीयन्ते मरणादयः |
महा-मुद्रां छ तेनैव वदन्ति विबुधोत्तमाः || १४ ||

iyaṃ khalu mahāmudrā mahā-siddhaiḥ pradarśitā |
mahā-kleśādayo doṣhāḥ kṣhīyante maraṇādayaḥ |
mahā-mudrāṃ cha tenaiva vadanti vibudhottamāḥ || 14 ||

Great evils and pains, like death, are destroyed by it, and for this reason wise men call it the Mahâ Mudrâ. 14.

छन्द्राङ्गे तु समभ्यस्य सूर्याङ्गे पुनरभ्यसेत |
यावत-तुल्या भवेत्सङ्ख्या ततो मुद्रां विसर्जयेत || १५ ||

chandrāngghe tu samabhyasya sūryāngghe punarabhyaset |
yāvat-tulyā bhavetsangkhyā tato mudrāṃ visarjayet || 15 ||

Having practised with the left nostril, it should be practised with the right one; and, when the number on both sides becomes equal, then the mudrâ should be discontinued. 15.

न हि पथ्यमपथ्यं वा रसाः सर्वे|अपि नीरसाः |
अपि भुक्तं विष्हं घोरं पीयूष्हमपि जीर्यति || १६ ||

na hi pathyamapathyaṃ vā rasāḥ sarve|api nīrasāḥ |
api bhuktaṃ viṣhaṃ ghoraṃ pīyūṣhamapi jīryati || 16 ||

There is nothing wholesome or injurious; for the practice of this mudrâ destroys the injurious effects of all the rasas (chemicals). Even the deadliest of poisons, if taken, acts like nectar. 16.

कष्हय-कुष्हठ-गुदावर्त-गुल्माजीर्ण-पुरोगमाः |
तस्य दोष्हाः कष्हयं यान्ति महामुद्रां तु यो|अभ्यसेत || १७ ||

kṣhaya-kuṣhṭha-ghudāvarta-ghulmājīrṇa-puroghamāḥ |
tasya doṣhāḥ kṣhayaṃ yānti mahāmudrāṃ tu yo|abhyaset || 17 ||

Consumption, leprosy, prolapsus anii, colic, and the diseases due to indigestion,—all these irregularities are removed by the practice of this Mahâ Mudrâ. 17.

कथितेयं महामुद्रा महा-सिद्धि-करा नृणाम |
गोपनीया परयत्नेन न देया यस्य कस्यछित || १८ ||

kathiteyaṃ mahāmudrā mahā-siddhi-karā nṝṇām |
ghopanīyā prayatnena na deyā yasya kasyachit || 18 ||

This Mahâ Mudrâ has been described as the giver of great success (Siddhi) to men. It should be kept secret by every effort, and not revealed to any and everyone. 18.

The Mahâ Bandha.

अथ महा-बन्धः
पार्ष्णिं वामस्य पादस्य योनि-सथाने नियोजयेत |
वामोरूपरि संस्थाप्य दक्ष्हिणं छरणं तथा || १९ ||

atha mahā-bandhaḥ
pārṣhṇiṃ vāmasya pādasya yoni-sthāne niyojayet |
vāmorūpari saṃsthāpya dakṣhiṇaṃ charaṇaṃ tathā || 19 ||

Press the left heel to the perineum and place the right foot on the left thigh. 19.

पूरयित्वा ततो वायुं हृदये छुबुकं दृढम |
निष्ह्पीड्यं वायुमाकुनछ्य मनो-मध्ये नियोजयेत || २० ||

pūrayitvā tato vāyuṃ hṝdaye chubukaṃ dṝḍham |
niṣhpīḍyaṃ vāyumākuñchya mano-madhye niyojayet || 20 ||

Fill in the air, keeping the chin firm against the chest, and, having pressed the air, the mind should he fixed on the middle of the eyebrows or in the suṣumnâ (the spine). 20.

धारयित्वा यथा-शक्ति रेछयेदनिलं शनैः |
सव्याङ्गे तु समभ्यस्य दक्ष्हाङ्गे पुनरभ्यसेत || २१ ||

dhārayitvā yathā-śakti rechayedanilaṃ śanaiḥ |
savyāngghe tu samabhyasya dakṣhāngghe punarabhyaset || 21 ||

Having kept it confined so long as possible, it should be expelled slowly. Having practised on the left side, it should be practised on the right side. 21.

मतमत्र तु केष्हांछित्कण्ठ-बन्धं विवर्जयेत |
राज-दन्त-सथ-जिह्वाया बन्धः शस्तो भवेदिति || २२ ||

matamatra tu keṣhāṃchitkaṇṭha-bandhaṃ vivarjayet |
rāja-danta-stha-jihvāyā bandhaḥ śasto bhavediti || 22 ||

Some are of opinion that the closing of throat is not necessary here, for keeping the tongue pressed against the roots of the upper teeth makes a good bandha (stop). 22.

अयं तु सर्व-नाडीनामूर्ध्वं गति-निरोधकः |
अयं खलु महा-बन्धो महा-सिद्धि-परदायकः || २३ ||

ayaṃ tu sarva-nāḍīnāmūrdhvaṃ ghati-nirodhakaḥ |
ayaṃ khalu mahā-bandho mahā-siddhi-pradāyakaḥ || 23 ||

This stops the upward motion of all the Nâdîs. Verily this Mahâ Bandha is the giver of great Siddhis. 23.

काल-पाश-महा-बन्ध-विमोछन-विछक्ष्हणः |

तरिवेणी-सङ्गमं धत्ते केदारं परापयेन्मनः || २४ ||

kāla-pāśa-mahā-bandha-vimochana-vichakṣhaṇaḥ |
triveṇī-sangghamaṃ dhatte kedāraṃ prāpayenmanaḥ || 24 ||

This Mahâ Bandha is the most skilful means for cutting away the snares of death. It brings about the conjunction of the Trivenî (Idâ, Pingalâ and Suṣumnâ) and carries the mind to Kedâr (the space between the eyebrows, which is the seat of Śiva). 24.

रूप-लावण्य-सम्पन्ना यथा सत्री पुरुष्हं विना |

महा-मुद्रा-महा-बन्धौ निष्ह्फलौ वेध-वर्जितौ || २५ ||

rūpa-lāvaṇya-sampannā yathā strī puruṣhaṃ vinā |
mahā-mudrā-mahā-bandhau niṣhphalau vedha-varjitau || 25 ||

As beauty and loveliness, do not avail a woman without husband, so the Mahâ Mudrâ and the Mahâ-Bandha are useless without the Mahâ Vedha. 25.

The Mahâ Vedha.

अथ महा-वेधः

महा-बन्ध-सथितो योगी कृत्वा पूरकमेक-धीः |

वायूनां गतिमावृत्य निभृतं कण्ठ-मुद्रया || २६ ||

atha mahā-vedhaḥ
mahā-bandha-sthito yoghī kṛtvā pūrakameka-dhīḥ |
vāyūnāṃ ghatimāvṛtya nibhṛtaṃ kaṇṭha-mudrayā || 26 ||

Sitting with Mahâ Bandha, the Yogî should fill in the air and keep his mind collected. The movements of the Vâyus (Prâṇa and Apâna) should be stopped by closing the throat.) 26.

सम-हस्त-युगो भूमौ सफिछौ सनाडयेछछनैः |

पुट-दवयमतिक्रम्य वायुः सफुरति मध्यगः || २७ ||

sama-hasta-yugho bhūmau sphichau sanāḍayechchanaiḥ |
puṭa-dvayamatikramya vāyuḥ sphurati madhyaghaḥ || 27 ||

Resting both the hands equally on the ground, he should raise himself a little and strike his buttocks against the ground gently.

The air, leaving both the passages (Idâ and Pingalâ), starts into the middle one. 27.

सोम-सूर्याग्नि-सम्बन्धो जायते छामृताय वै |
मृतावस्था समुत्पन्ना ततो वायुं विरेछयेत || २८ ||

soma-sūryāghni-sambandho jāyate chāmṛtāya vai |
mṛtāvasthā samutpannā tato vāyuṃ virechayet || 28 ||

The union of the Idâ and the Pingalâ is effected, in order to bring about immortality. When the air becomes as it were dead (by leaving its course through the Idâ and the Pingalâ) (*i.e.*, when it has been kept confined), then it should be expelled. 28.

महा-वेधो|अयमभ्यासान्महा-सिद्धि-परदायकः |
वली-पलित-वेप-घनः सेव्यते साधकोत्तमैः || २९ ||

mahā-vedho|ayamabhyāsānmahā-siddhi-pradāyakaḥ |
valī-palita-vepa-ghnaḥ sevyate sādhakottamaiḥ || 29 ||

The practice of this Mahâ Vedha, the giver of great Siddhis, destroys old age, grey hair, and shaking of the body, and therefore it is practised by the best masters. 29.

एतत्त्रयं महा-गुह्यं जरा-मृत्यु-विनाशनम |
वह्नि-वृद्धि-करं छैव हयणिमादि-गुण-परदम || ३० ||

etattrayaṃ mahā-ghuhyaṃ jarā-mṛtyu-vināśanam |
vahni-vṛddhi-karaṃ chaiva hyaṇimādi-ghuṇa-pradam || 30 ||

These THREE are the great secrets. They are the destroyers of old age and death, increase the appetite, confer the accomplishments of Anima, etc. 30.

अष्ह्टधा करियते छैव यामे यामे दिने दिने |
पुण्य-संभार-सन्धाय पापौघ-भिदुरं सदा |
सम्यक-शिक्ष्हावतामेवं सवल्पं परथम-साधनम || ३१ ||

aṣhṭadhā kriyate chaiva yāme yāme dine dine |
puṇya-saṃbhāra-sandhāya pāpaugha-bhiduraṃ sadā |
samyak-śikṣhāvatāmevaṃ svalpaṃ prathama-sādhanam || 31 ||

They should, be practised in 8 ways, daily and hourly. They increase collection of good actions and lessen the evil ones. People, instructed well, should begin their practice, little by little, first. 31.

The Khechari.

अथ खेछरी कपाल-कुहरे जिहवा परविष्हटा विपरीतगगा | भरुवोरन्तर्गता दृष्हिटर्मुद्रा भवति खेछरी || ३२ ||

atha khecharī kapāla-kuhare jihvā praviṣhṭā viparītaghā | bhruvorantarghatā dṛṣhṭirmudrā bhavati khecharī || 32 ||

The Khechari Mudrâ is accomplished by thrusting the tongue into the gullet, by turning it over itself, and keeping the eyesight in the middle of the eyebrows. 32.

छेदन-छालन-दोहैः कलां करमेणाथ वर्धयेत्तावत | सा यावद्भ्रू-मध्यं सपृशति तदा खेछरी-सिद्धिः || ३३ ||

chedana-chālana-dohaiḥ kalāṃ krameṇātha vardhayettāvat | sā yāvadbhrū-madhyaṃ spṛśati tadā khecharī-siddhiḥ || 33 ||

To accomplish this, the tongue is lengthened by cutting the frænum linguæ, moving, and pulling it. When it can touch the space between the eyebrows, then Khechari can be accomplished. 33.

सनुही-पत्र-निभं शस्त्रं सुतीक्ष्हणं सनिग्ध-निर्मलम | समादाय ततस्तेन रोम-मात्रं समुछिछनेत || ३४ ||

snuhī-patra-nibhaṃ śastraṃ sutīkṣhṇaṃ snighdha-nirmalam | samādāya tatastena roma-mātraṃ samuchchinet || 34 ||

Taking a sharp, smooth, and clean instrument, of the shape of a cactus leaf, the frænum of the tongue should be cut a little (as much as a hair's thickness), at a time. 34.

ततः सैन्धव-पथ्याभ्यां छूर्णिताभ्यां परघर्ष्हयेत | पुनः सप्त-दिने पराप्ते रोम-मात्रं समुछिछनेत || ३५ ||

tataḥ saindhava-pathyābhyāṃ chūrṇitābhyāṃ pragharṣhayet | punaḥ sapta-dine prāpte roma-mātraṃ samuchchinet || 35 ||

Then rock salt and yellow myrobalan (both powdered) should be rubbed in. On the 7th day, it should again be cut a hair's breadth. 35.

एवं करमेण षहण-मासं नित्यं युक्तः समाछरेत | षहण्मासाद्रसना-मूल-शिरा-बन्धः परणश्यति || ३६ ||

evaṃ krameṇa ṣhaṇ-māsaṃ nityaṃ yuktaḥ samācharet | ṣhaṇmāsādrasanā-mūla-śirā-bandhaḥ praṇaśyati || 36 ||

One should go on doing thus, regularly for six months. At the end of six months, the frænum of the tongue will be completely cut. 36.

कलां पराङ्मुखीं कृत्वा तरिपथे परियोजयेत | सा भवेत्खेछरी मुद्रा वयोम-छक्रं तदुछ्यते || ३७ ||

kalāṃ parāngmukhīṃ kṛtvā tripathe pariyojayet | sā bhavetkhecharī mudrā vyoma-chakraṃ taduchyate || 37 ||

Turning the tongue upwards, it is fixed on the three ways (œsophagus, windpipe and palate.) Thus it makes the Khechari Mudrâ, and is called the Vyoma Chakra. 37.

रसनामूर्ध्वगां कृत्वा कष्हणार्धमपि तिष्हठति | विष्हैर्विमुछ्यते योगी वयाधि-मृत्यु-जरादिभिः || ३८ ||

rasanāmūrdhvaghāṃ kṛtvā kṣhaṇārdhamapi tiṣhṭhati | viṣhairvimuchyate yoghī vyādhi-mṛtyu-jarādibhiḥ || 38 ||

The Yogî who sits for a minute turning his tongue upwards, is saved from poisons, diseases, death, old age, etc. 38.

न रोगो मरणं तन्द्रा न निद्रा न कष्हुधा तृष्हा | न छ मूर्छ्छा भवेत्तस्य यो मुद्रां वेत्ति खेछरीम || ३९ ||

na rogho maraṇaṃ tandrā na nidrā na kṣhudhā tṛṣhā | na cha mūrchchā bhavettasya yo mudrāṃ vetti khecharīm || 39 ||

He who knows the Khechari Mudrâ is not afflicted with disease, death, sloth, sleep, hunger, thirst, and swooning. 39.

पीड्यते न स रोगेण लिप्यते न छ कर्मणा |
बाध्यते न स कालेन यो मुद्रां वेत्ति खेछरीम || ४० ||

pīḍyate na sa roghena lipyate na cha karmaṇā |
bādhyate na sa kālena yo mudrāṃ vetti khecharīm || 40 ||

He who knows the Khechari Mudrâ, is not troubled by diseases, is not stained with karmas, and is not snared by time. 40.

छित्तं छरति खे यस्माज्जिह्वा छरति खे गता |
तेनैष्हा खेछरी नाम मुद्रा सिद्धैर्निरूपिता || ४१ ||

chittaṃ charati khe yasmājjihvā charati khe ghatā |
tenaiṣhā khecharī nāma mudrā siddhairnirūpitā || 41 ||

खेछर्या मुद्रितं येन विवरं लम्बिकोर्ध्वतः |
न तस्य कष्हरते बिन्दुः कामिन्याः शलेष्हितस्य छ || ४२ ||

khecharyā mudritaṃ yena vivaraṃ lambikordhvataḥ |
na tasya kṣharate binduḥ kāminyāḥ śleṣhitasya cha || 42 ||

The Siddhas have devised this Khechari Mudrâ from the fact that the mind and the tongue reach âkâśa by its practice. 41.

छलितो|अपि यदा बिन्दुः सम्प्राप्तो योनि-मण्डलम |
वरजत्यूर्ध्वं हृतः शक्त्या निबद्धो योनि-मुद्रया || ४३ ||

chalito|api yadā binduḥ samprāpto yoni-maṇḍalam |
vrajatyūrdhvaṃ hṛtaḥ śaktyā nibaddho yoni-mudrayā || 43 ||

If the hole behind the palate be stopped with Khechari by turning the tongue upwards, then bindu cannot leave its place even if a woman were embraced. 42.

ऊर्ध्व-जिह्वः सथिरो भूत्वा सोमपानं करोति यः |
मासार्धेन न सन्देहो मृत्युं जयति योगवित || ४४ ||

ūrdhva-jihvaḥ sthiro bhūtvā somapānaṃ karoti yaḥ |
māsārdhena na sandeho mṛtyuṃ jayati yoghavit || 44 ||

If the Yogî drinks Somarasa (juice) by sitting with the tongue turned backwards and mind concentrated, there is no doubt he conquers death within 15 days. 43.

नित्यं सोम-कला-पूर्णं शरीरं यस्य योगिनः |
तक्ष्हकेणापि दष्ह्टस्य विष्हं तस्य न सर्पति || ४५ ||

nityaṃ soma-kalā-pūrṇaṃ śarīraṃ yasya yoghinaḥ |
takṣhakeṇāpi daṣhṭasya viṣhaṃ tasya na sarpati || 45 ||

If the Yogî, whose body is full of Somarasa (juice), were bitten by Takshaka (snake), its poison cannot permeate his body. 44.

As fire is inseparably connected with the wood and light is connected with the wick and oil, so does the soul not leave the body full of nectar exuding from the Soma. 45.

Note.—Soma (Chandra) is described later on located in the thousand-petalled lotus in the human brain, and is the same as is seen on Śivas' head in pictures, and from which a sort of juice exudes. It is the retaining of this exudation which makes one immortal.

इन्धनानि यथा वह्निस्तैल-वर्ति छ दीपकः |
तथा सोम-कला-पूर्णं देही देहं न मुनछति || ४६ ||

indhanāni yathā vahnistaila-varti cha dīpakaḥ |
tathā soma-kalā-pūrṇaṃ dehī dehaṃ na muñchati || 46 ||

Those who eat the flesh of the cow and drink the immortal liquor daily, are regarded by me men of noble family. Others are but a disgrace to their families. 46.

Translation: Fortunate are the parents and blessed is the country and the family where a Yogî is born. Anything given to such a Yogî, becomes immortal. One, who discriminates between Puruṣa and Prakṛiti, purges the sins of a million incarnations, by seeing, speaking, and touching such men (*i.e.*, Yogî.)

A Yogî far exceeds a thousand householders, a hundred vânaprasthas, and a thousand Brahmacharîs.

Who can know the reality of the Raja Yoga? That country is very sacred where resides a man who knows it. By seeing and honouring him, generations of ignorant men get mokṣa, what to speak of those who are actually engaged in it. He who knows internal and external yoga, deserves adoration from you and me, what if he is adored by the rest of mankind!

Those who engage in the great yoga, once, twice or thrice daily, are to be known as masters of great wealth (maheshwaras) or Lords.

गोमांसं भक्ष्हयेन्नित्यं पिबेदमर-वारुणीम |
कुलीनं तमहं मन्ये छेतरे कुल-घातकाः || ४७ ||

ghomāṃsaṃ bhakṣhayennityaṃ pibedamara-vāruṇīm |
kulīnaṃ tamahaṃ manye chetare kula-ghātakāḥ || 47 ||

गो-शब्देनोदिता जिह्वा तत्प्रवेशो हि तालुनि |
गो-मांस-भक्ष्हणं तत्तु महा-पातक-नाशनम || ४८ ||

gho-śabdenoditā jihvā tatpraveśo hi tāluni |
gho-māṃsa-bhakṣhaṇaṃ tattu mahā-pātaka-nāśanam || 48 ||

The word गी means tongue; eating it is thrusting it in the gullet which destroys great sins. 47.

जिह्वा-परवेश-सम्भूत-वह्निनोत्पादितः खलु |
छन्द्रात्स्रवति यः सारः सा सयादमर-वारुणी || ४९ ||

jihvā-praveśa-sambhūta-vahninotpāditaḥ khalu |
chandrātsravati yaḥ sāraḥ sā syādamara-vāruṇī || 49 ||

Immortal liquor is the nectar exuding from the moon (Chandra situated on the left side of the space between the eyebrows). It is produced by the fire which is generated by thrusting the tongue. 48.

छुम्बन्ती यदि लम्बिकाग्रमनिशं जिह्वा-रस-सयन्दिनी
स-कष्हारा कटुकाम्ल-दुग्ध-सदृशी मध्वाज्य-तुल्या तथा |
वयाधीनां हरणं जरान्त-करणं शस्त्रागमोदीरणं
तस्य सयादमरत्वमष्ह्ट-गुणितं सिद्धाङ्गनाकर्ष्हणम || ५० ||

chumbantī yadi lambikāghramaniśaṃ jihvā-rasa-syandinī
sa-kṣhārā kaṭukāmla-dughdha-sadṝśī madhvājya-tulyā tathā |
vyādhīnāṃ haraṇaṃ jarānta-karaṇaṃ śastrāghamodīraṇaṃ
tasya syādamaratvamaṣhṭa-ghuṇitaṃ siddhāngghanākarṣhaṇam || 50 ||

If the tongue can touch with its end the hole from which falls the rasa (juice) which is saltish, bitter, sour, milky and similar to ghee and honey, one can drive away disease, destroy old age, can evade an attack of arms, become immortal in eight ways and can attract fairies. 49.

ऊर्द्व्हास्यो रसनां नियम्य विवरे शक्तिं परां छिन्तयन | उत्कल्लोल-कला-जलं छ विमलं धारामयं यः पिबेन निर्व्याधिः स मृणाल-कोमल-वपुर्योगी छिरं जीवति || ५१ ||

ūrdvhāsyo rasanāṃ niyamya vivare śaktiṃ parāṃ chintayan | utkallola-kalā-jalaṃ cha vimalaṃ dhārāmayaṃ yaḥ piben nirvyādhiḥ sa mṛṇāla-komala-vapuryoghī chiraṃ jīvati || 51 ||

He who drinks the clear stream of liquor of the moon (soma) falling from the brain to the sixteen-petalled lotus (in the heart), obtained by means of Prâṇa, by applying the tongue to the hole of the pendant in the palate, and by meditating on the great power (Kuṇḍalinî), becomes free from disease and tender in body, like the stalk of a lotus, and the Yogî lives a very long life. 50.

यत्प्रालेयं परहित-सुष्हिरं मेरु-मूर्धान्तर-सथं तस्मिंस्तत्त्वं परवदति सुधीस्तन-मुखं निम्नगानाम | छन्द्रात्सारः सरवति वपुष्हस्तेन मृत्युर्नराणां तद्बध्नीयात्सुकरणमधो नान्यथा काय-सिद्धिः || ५२ ||

yatprāleyaṃ prahita-suṣhiraṃ meru-mūrdhāntara-sthaṃ tasmiṃstattvaṃ pravadati sudhīstan-mukhaṃ nimnaghānām | chandrātsāraḥ sravati vapuṣhastena mṛtyurnarāṇāṃ tadbadhnīyātsukaraṇamadho nānyathā kāya-siddhiḥ || 52 ||

On the top of the Merû (vertebral column), concealed in a hole, is the Somarasa (nectar of Chandra); the wise, whose intellect is not overpowered by Raja and Tama guṇas, but in whom Satwa guṇa is predominant, say there is the (universal spirit) âtma in it. It is the source of the down-going Idâ, Pingalâ and Suṣumnâ Nâdis, which are the Ganges, the Yamuna and the Sarasvati. From that Chandra is shed the essence of the body which causes death of men. It should, therefore, be stopped from shedding. This (Khechari Mudrâ) is a very good instrument for this purpose. There is no other means of achieving this end. 51.

सुष्हिरं जञान-जनकं पञ्छ-सरोतः-समन्वितम | तिष्ह्ठते खेछरी मुद्रा तस्मिन्शून्ये निरञ्जने || ५३ ||

suṣhiraṃ jñāna-janakaṃ pañcha-srotaḥ-samanvitam | tiṣhṭhate khecharī mudrā tasminśūnye nirañjane || 53 ||

This hole is the generator of knowledge and is the source of the five streams (Idâ, Pingalâ, &c.). In that colorless vacuum, Khecharî Mudrâ should be established. 52.

एकं सृष्टिमयं बीजमेका मुद्रा छ खेछरी |
एको देवो निरालम्ब एकावस्था मनोन्मनी || ५४ ||

ekaṃ sṛṣhṭimayaṃ bījamekā mudrā cha khecharī |
eko devo nirālamba ekāvasthā manonmanī || 54 ||

There is only one seed germinating the whole universe from it; and there is only one Mudrâ, called Khecharî. There is only one deva (god) without any one's support, and there is one condition called Manonmaṇi. 53.

The Uḍḍiyâna Bandha.

Uḍḍiyâna is so called by the Yogîs, because by its practice the Prâṇa (Vâyu,) flies (flows) in the Suṣumnâ. 54.

अथ उड्डीयान-बन्धः
बद्धो येन सुष्हुम्णायां पराणस्तूड्डीयते यतः |
तस्मादुड्डीयनाख्यो|अयं योगिभिः समुदाहृतः || ५५ ||

atha uḍḍīyāna-bandhaḥ
baddho yena suṣhumṇāyāṃ prāṇastūḍḍīyate yataḥ |
tasmāduḍḍīyanākhyo|ayaṃ yoghibhiḥ samudāhṛtaḥ || 55 ||

Uḍḍiyâna is so called, because the great bird, Prâṇa, tied to it, flies without being fatigued. It is explained below. 55.

उड्डीनं कुरुते यस्मादविश्रान्तं महा-खगः |
उड्डीयानं तदेव सयात्तव बन्धो|अभिधीयते || ५६ ||

uḍḍīnaṃ kurute yasmādaviśrāntaṃ mahā-khaghaḥ |
uḍḍīyānaṃ tadeva syāttava bandho|abhidhīyate || 56 ||

उदरे पश्छिमं तानं नाभेरूर्ध्वं छ कारयेत |
उड्डीयानो हयसौ बन्धो मृत्यु-मातङ्ग-केसरी || ५७ ||

udare paśchimaṃ tānaṃ nābherūrdhvaṃ cha kārayet |
uḍḍīyāno hyasau bandho mṛtyu-mātanggha-kesarī || 57 ||

The belly above the navel is pressed backwards towards the spine. This Uḍḍiyâna Bandha is like a lion for the elephant of death. 56.

उड्डीयानं तु सहजं गुरुणा कथितं सदा |
अभ्यसेत्सततं यस्तु वृद्धो|अपि तरुणायते || ५८ ||

uḍḍīyānaṃ tu sahajaṃ ghuruṇā kathitaṃ sadā |
abhyasetsatataṃ yastu vṛddho|api taruṇāyate || 58 ||

Uḍḍiyâna is always very easy, when learnt from a guru. The practiser of this, if old, becomes young again. 57.

The portions above and below the navel, should be drawn backwards towards the spine. By practising this for six months one can undoubtedly conquer death. 58.

नाभेरूर्ध्वमधश्छापि तानं कुर्यात्प्रयत्नतः |
षहण्गारागभ्यरोन्गृत्युं जयत्येव न रांशयः || ५९ ||

nābherūrdhvamadhaśchāpi tānaṃ kuryātprayatnataḥ |
ṣhaṇmāsamabhyasenmṛtyuṃ jayatyeva na saṃśayaḥ || 59 ||

सर्वेष्हामेव बन्धानां उत्तमो हयुड्डीयानकः |
उड्डियाने दृढे बन्धे मुक्तिः सवाभाविकी भवेत || ६० ||

sarveṣhāmeva bandhānāṃ uttamo hyuḍḍīyānakaḥ |
uḍḍiyāne dṛḍhe bandhe muktiḥ svābhāvikī bhavet || 60 ||

Of all the Bandhas, Uḍḍiyâna is the best; for by binding it firmly liberation comes spontaneously. 59.

The Mûla Bandha.

Pressing Yoni (perineum) with the heel, contract up the anus. By drawing the Apâna thus, Mûla Bandha is made. 60.

अथ मूल-बन्धः
पार्ष्ण्-भागेन सम्पीड्य योनिमाकुनछयेद्गुदम |
अपानमूर्ध्वमाकृष्हय मूल-बन्धो|अभिधीयते || ६१ ||

atha mūla-bandhaḥ
pārṣhṇi-bhāghena sampīḍya yonimākuñchayedghudam |
apānamūrdhvamākṝṣhya mūla-bandho|abhidhīyate || 61 ||

The Apâna, naturally inclining downward, is made to go up by force. This Mûla Bandha is spoken of by Yogîs as done by contracting the anus. 61.

अधो-गतिमपानं वा ऊर्ध्वगं कुरुते बलात |
आकुनछनेन तं पराहुर्मूल-बन्धं हि योगिनः || ६२ ||

adho-ghatimapānaṃ vā ūrdhvaghaṃ kurute balāt |
ākuñchanena taṃ prāhurmūla-bandhaṃ hi yoghinaḥ || 62 ||

Pressing the heel well against the anus, draw up the air by force, again and again till it (air) goes up. 62.

गुदं पाष्र्ण्या तु सम्पीड्य वायुमाकुनछयेद्बलात |
वारं वारं यथा छोर्ध्वं समायाति समीरणः || ६३ ||

ghudaṃ pārṣhṇyā tu sampīḍya vāyumākuñchayedbalāt |
vāraṃ vāraṃ yathā chordhvaṃ samāyāti samīraṇaḥ || 63 ||

Prâṇa, Apâna, Nâda and Bindu uniting into one in this way, give success in Yoga, undoubtedly. 63.

पराणापानौ नाद-बिन्दू मूल-बन्धेन छैकताम |
गत्वा योगस्य संसिद्धिं यछछतो नात्र संशयः || ६४ ||

prāṇāpānau nāda-bindū mūla-bandhena chaikatām |
ghatvā yoghasya saṃsiddhiṃ yachchato nātra saṃśayaḥ || 64 ||

By the purification of Prâṇa, and Apâna, urine and excrements decrease. Even an old man becomes young by constantly practising Mûla Bandha. 64.

अपान-पराणयोरैक्यं कष्हयो मूत्र-पुरीष्हयोः |
युवा भवति वृद्धो|अपि सततं मूल-बन्धनात || ६५ ||

apāna-prāṇayoraikyaṃ kṣhayo mūtra-purīṣhayoḥ |
yuvā bhavati vṝddho|api satataṃ mūla-bandhanāt || 65 ||

Going up, the Apâna enters the zone of fire, *i.e.*, the stomach. The flame of fire struck by the air is thereby lengthened. 65.

In the centre of the body is the seat of fire, like heated gold.

In men it is triangular, in quadrupeds square, in birds circular. There is a long thin flame in this fire.

It is gastric fire.

अपान ऊर्ध्वगे जाते परयाते वह्नि-मण्डलम | तदानल-शिखा दीर्घा जायते वायुनाहता || ६६ ||

apāna ūrdhvaghe jāte prayāte vahni-maṇḍalam | tadānala-śikhā dīrghā jāyate vāyunāhatā || 66 ||

These, fire and Apâna, go to the naturally hot Prâṇa, which, becoming inflamed thereby, causes burning sensation in the body. 66.

ततो यातो वह्न्य-अपानौ पराणमुष्ह्ण-सवरूपकम | तेनात्यन्त-परदीप्तस्तु जवलनो देहजस्तथा || ६७ ||

tato yāto vahny-apānau prāṇamuṣhṇa-svarūpakam | tenātyanta-pradīptastu jvalano dehajastathā || 67 ||

The Kuṇḍalinî, which has been sleeping all this time, becomes well heated by this means and awakens well. It becomes straight like a serpent, struck dead with a stick. 67.

तेन कुण्डलिनी सुप्ता सन्तप्ता सम्प्रबुध्यते | दण्डाहता भुजङ्गीव निश्वस्य ऋजुतां वरजेत || ६८ ||

tena kuṇḍalinī suptā santaptā samprabudhyate | daṇḍāhatā bhujangghīva niśvasya ṛjutāṃ vrajet || 68 ||

It enters the Brahma Nâdî, just as a serpent enters its hole. Therefore, the Yogî should always practise this Mûla Bandha. 68.

बिलं परविष्हटेव ततो बरह्म-नाड्यं तरं वरजेत | तस्मान्नित्यं मूल-बन्धः कर्तव्यो योगिभिः सदा || ६९ ||

bilaṃ praviṣhṭeva tato brahma-nāḍyaṃ taraṃ vrajet | tasmānnityaṃ mūla-bandhaḥ kartavyo yoghibhiḥ sadā || 69 ||

The Jâlandhara Bandha.

अथ जलन्धर-बन्धः
कण्ठमाकुनछय हृदये सथापयेछ्छिबुकं दृढम |
बन्धो जालन्धराख्यो|अयं जरा-मृत्यु-विनाशकः || ७० ||

atha jalandhara-bandhaḥ
kaṇṭhamākuñchya hṛdaye sthāpayechchibukaṃ dṛḍham |
bandho jālandharākhyo|ayaṃ jarā-mṛtyu-vināśakaḥ || 70 ||

Contract the throat and press the chin firmly against the chest. This is called Jâlandhara Bandha, which destroys old age and death. 69.

बध्नाति हि सिराजालमधो-गामि नभो-जलम |
ततो जालन्धरो बन्धः कण्ठ-दुःखौघ-नाशनः || ७१ ||

badhnāti hi sirājālamadho-ghāmi nabho-jalam |
tato jālandharo bandhaḥ kaṇṭha-duḥkhaugha-nāśanaḥ || 71 ||

It stops the opening (hole) of the group of the Nâdîs, through which the juice from the sky (from the Soma or Chandra in the brain) falls down. It is, therefore, called the Jâlandhara Bandha — the destroyer of a host of diseases of the throat. 70.

जालन्धरे कृते बन्धे कण्ठ-संकोछ-लक्ष्हणे |
न पीयूष्हं पतत्यग्नौ न छ वायुः परकुप्यति || ७२ ||

jālandhare kṛte bandhe kaṇṭha-saṃkocha-lakṣhaṇe |
na pīyūṣhaṃ patatyaghnau na cha vāyuḥ prakupyati || 72 ||

In Jâlandhara Bandha, the indications of a perfect contraction of throat are, that the nectar does not fall into the fire (the Sûrya situated in the navel), and the air is not disturbed. 71.

कण्ठ-संकोछनेनैव दवे नाड्यौ सतम्भयेद्दृढम |
मध्य-छक्रमिदं जञेयं षहोडशाधार-बन्धनम || ७३ ||

kaṇṭha-saṃkochanenaiva dve nāḍyau stambhayeddṛḍham |
madhya-chakramidaṃ jñeyaṃ ṣhoḍaśādhāra-bandhanam || 73 ||

The two Nâdîs should be stopped firmly by contracting the throat. This is called the middle circuit or centre (Madhya Chakra), and it stops the 16 âdhâras (*i.e.*, vital parts). 72.

The sixteen vital parts mentioned by renowned Yogîs are the (1) thumbs, (2) ankles, (3) knees, (4) thighs, (5) the prepuce, (6) organs of generation, (17) the navel, (8) the heart, (9) the neck, (10) the throat, (11) the palate, (12) the nose, (13) the middle of the eyebrows, (14) the forehead, (15) the head and (16) the Brahma randhra.

मूल-सथानं समाकुनछ्य उड्डियानं तु कारयेत |
इडां छ पिङ्गलां बद्ध्वा वाहयेत्पश्छिमे पथि || ७४ ||

mūla-sthānaṃ samākuñchya uḍḍiyānaṃ tu kārayet |
iḍāṃ cha pingghalāṃ baddhvā vāhayetpaśchime pathi || 74 ||

By drawing up the mûlasthâna (anus,) Uḍḍiyâna Bandha should be performed. The flow of the air should be directed to the Suṣumnâ, by closing the Idâ, and the Pingalâ. 73.

अनेनैव विधानेन परयाति पवनो लयम |
ततो न जायते मृत्युर्जरा-रोगादिकं तथा || ७५ ||

anenaiva vidhānena prayāti pavano layam |
tato na jāyate mṛtyurjarā-roghādikaṃ tathā || 75 ||

The Prâna becomes calm and latent by this means, and thus there is no death, old age, disease, etc. 74.

बन्ध-तरयमिदं शरेष्ह्ठं महा-सिद्धैश्छ सेवितम |
सर्वेष्हां हठ-तन्त्राणां साधनं योगिनो विदुः || ७६ ||

bandha-trayamidaṃ śreṣhṭhaṃ mahā-siddhaiścha sevitam |
sarveṣhāṃ haṭha-tantrāṇāṃ sādhanaṃ yoghino viduḥ || 76 ||

These three Bandhas are the best of all and have been practised by the masters. Of all the means of success in the Haṭha Yoga, they are known to the Yogîs as the chief ones. 75.

यत्किंछित्स्रवते छन्द्रादमृतं दिव्य-रूपिणः |
तत्सर्वं गरसते सूर्यस्तेन पिण्डो जरायुतः || ७७ ||

yatkiṃchitsravate chandrādamṛtaṃ divya-rūpiṇaḥ |
tatsarvaṃ ghrasate sūryastena piṇḍo jarāyutaḥ || 77 ||

The whole of the nectar, possessing divine qualities, which exudes from the Soma (Chandra) is devoured by the Sûrya; and, owing to this, the body becomes old. 76.

To remedy this, the opening of the Sûrya is avoided by excellent means. It is to be learnt best by instructions from a guru; but not by even a million discussions. 77.

The Viparîta Karaṇî.

अथ विपरीत-करणी मुद्रा
तत्रास्ति करणं दिव्यं सूर्यस्य मुख-वञ्छनम |
गुरूपदेशतो जञेयं न तु शास्त्रार्थ-कोटिभिः || ७८ ||

atha viparīta-karaṇī mudrā
tatrāsti karaṇaṃ divyaṃ sūryasya mukha-vañchanam |
ghurūpadeśato jñeyaṃ na tu śāstrārtha-koṭibhiḥ || 78 ||

Above the navel and below the palate respectively, are the Sûrya and the Chandra. The exercise, called the Viparîta Karaṇî, is learnt from the guru's instructions. 78.

ऊर्ध्व-नाभेरधस्तालोरूर्ध्वं भानुरधः शशी |
करणी विपरीताखा गुरु-वाक्येन लभ्यते || ७९ ||

ūrdhva-nābheradhastālorūrdhvaṃ bhānuradhaḥ śaśī |
karaṇī viparītākhā ghuru-vākyena labhyate || 79 ||

This exercise increases the appetite; and, therefore, one who practises it, should obtain a good supply of food. If the food be scanty, it will burn him at once. 79.

नित्यमभ्यास-युक्तस्य जठराग्नि-विवर्धनी |
आहारो बहुलस्तस्य सम्पाद्यः साधकस्य छ || ८० ||

nityamabhyāsa-yuktasya jaṭharāghni-vivardhanī |
āhāro bahulastasya sampādyaḥ sādhakasya cha || 80 ||

Place the head on the ground and the feet up into the sky, for a second only the first day, and increase this time daily. 80.

अल्पाहारो यदि भवेदग्निर्दहति तत-कष्हणात |
अधः-शिराश्छोर्ध्व-पादः कष्हणं सयात्प्रथमे दिने || ८१ ||

alpāhāro yadi bhavedaghnirdahati tat-kṣhaṇāt |
adhaḥ-śirāśchordhva-pādaḥ kṣhaṇaṃ syātprathame dine || 81 ||

कष्हणाछ्छ किंछिदधिकमभ्यसेछ्छ दिने दिने |
वलितं पलितं छैव षहण्मासोर्ध्वं न दृश्यते |
याम-मात्रं तु यो नित्यमभ्यसेत्स तु कालजित || ८२ ||

kṣhaṇāchcha kiṃchidadhikamabhyasechcha dine dine |
valitaṃ palitaṃ chaiva ṣhaṇmāsordhvaṃ na dṝśyate |
yāma-mātraṃ tu yo nityamabhyasetsa tu kālajit || 82 ||

After six months, the wrinkles and grey hair are not seen. He who practises it daily, even for two hours, conquers death. 81.

The Vajrolî.

अथ वज्रोली
सवेछ्छया वर्तमानो|अपि योगोक्तैर्नियमैर्विना |
वज्रोलीं यो विजानाति स योगी सिद्धि-भाजनम || ८३ ||

atha vajrolī
svechchayā vartamāno|api yoghoktairniyamairvinā |
vajrolīṃ yo vijānāti sa yoghī siddhi-bhājanam || 83 ||

Even if one who lives a wayward life, without observing any rules of Yoga, but performs Vajrolî, deserves success and is a Yogî. 82.

तत्र वस्तु-दवयं वक्ष्हये दुर्लभं यस्य कस्यछित |
कष्हीरं छैकं दवितीयं तु नारी छ वश-वर्तिनी || ८४ ||

tatra vastu-dvayaṃ vakṣhye durlabhaṃ yasya kasyachit |
kṣhīraṃ chaikaṃ dvitīyaṃ tu nārī cha vaśa-vartinī || 84 ||

Two things are necessary for this, and these are difficult to get for the ordinary people—(1) milk and (2) a woman behaving, as desired. 83.

मेहनेन शनैः सम्यगूर्ध्वाकुनछनमभ्यसेत |
पुरुष्हो|अप्यथवा नारी वज्रोली-सिद्धिमाप्नुयात || ८५ ||

mehanena śanaiḥ samyaghūrdhvākuñchanamabhyaset |
puruṣho|apyathavā nārī vajrolī-siddhimāpnuyāt || 85 ||

By practising to draw in the *bindu*, discharged during cohabitation, whether one be a man or a woman, one obtains success in the practice of Vajrolî. 84.

यत्नतः शस्त-नालेन फूत्कारं वज्र-कन्दरे |
शनैः शनैः परकुर्वीत वायु-संछार-कारणात || ८६ ||

yatnataḥ śasta-nālena phūtkāraṃ vajra-kandare |
śanaiḥ śanaiḥ prakurvīta vāyu-saṃchāra-kāraṇāt || 86 ||

By means of a pipe, one should blow air slowly into the passage in the male organ. 85.

नारी-भगे पदद-बिन्दुमभ्यासेनोर्ध्वमाहरेत |
छलितं छ निजं बिन्दुमूर्ध्वमाकृष्ह्य रक्ष्हयेत || ८७ ||

nārī-bhaghe padad-bindumabhyāsenordhvamāharet |
chalitaṃ cha nijaṃ bindumūrdhvamākṝṣhya rakṣhayet || 87 ||

By practice, the discharged *bindu* is drawn out. One can draw back and preserve one's own discharged bindu. 86.

एवं संरक्ष्हयेद्बिन्दुं जयति योगवित |
मरणं बिन्दु-पातेन जीवनं बिन्दु-धारणात || ८८ ||

evaṃ saṃrakṣhayedbinduṃ jayati yoghavit |
maraṇaṃ bindu-pātena jīvanaṃ bindu-dhāraṇāt || 88 ||

The Yogî who can protect his *bindu* thus, overcomes death; because death comes by discharging *bindu*, and life is prolonged by its preservation. 87.

सुगन्धो योगिनो देहे जायते बिन्दु-धारणात |
यावद्बिन्दुः सथिरो देहे तावत्काल-भयं कुतः || ८९ ||

sughandho yoghino dehe jāyate bindu-dhāraṇāt |
yāvadbinduḥ sthiro dehe tāvatkāla-bhayaṃ kutaḥ || 89 ||

By preserving *bindu*, the body of the Yogî emits a pleasing smell. There is no fear of death, so long as the *bindu* is well-established in the body. 88.

छित्तायत्तं नृणां शुक्रं शुक्रायत्तं छ जीवितम |
तस्माछ्छुक्रं मनश्छैव रक्ष्हणीयं परयत्नतः || ९० ||

chittāyattaṃ nṝṇāṃ śukraṃ śukrāyattaṃ cha jīvitam |
tasmāchchukraṃ manaśchaiva rakṣhaṇīyaṃ prayatnataḥ || 90 ||

ऋतुमत्या रजो|अप्येवं निजं बिन्दुं छ रक्ष्हयेत |
मेढ्रेणाकर्ष्हयेदूर्ध्वं सम्यगभ्यास-योग-वित || ९१ ||

ṛtumatyā rajo|apyevaṃ nijaṃ binduṃ cha rakṣhayet |
meḍhreṇākarṣhayedūrdhvaṃ samyaghabhyāsa-yogha-vit || 91 ||

The *bindu* of men is under the control of the mind, and life is dependent on the *bindu*. Hence, mind and *bindu* should be protected by all means. 89.

The Sahajolî.

अथ सहजोलिः
सहजोलिश्छामरोलिर्वज्रोल्या भेद एकतः |
जले सुभस्म निक्ष्हिप्य दग्ध-गोमय-सम्भवम || ९२ ||

atha sahajoliḥ
sahajoliśchāmarolirvajrolyā bheda ekataḥ |
jale subhasma nikṣhipya daghdha-ghomaya-sambhavam || 92 ||

Sahajolî and Amarolî are only the different kinds of Vajrolî. Ashes from burnt up cowdung should be mixed with water. 90.

वज्रोली-मैथुनादूर्ध्वं सत्री-पुंसोः सवाङ्ग-लेपनम |
आसीनयोः सुखेनैव मुक्त-वयापारयोः कष्हणात || ९३ ||

vajrolī-maithunādūrdhvaṃ strī-puṃsoḥ svānggha-lepanam |
āsīnayoḥ sukhenaiva mukta-vyāpārayoḥ kṣhaṇāt || 93 ||

Being free from the exercise of Vajrolî, man and woman should both rub it on their bodies. 91.

सहजोलिरियं परोक्ता शरद्धेया योगिभिः सदा |
अयं शुभकरो योगो भोग-युक्तो|अपि मुक्तिदः || ९४ ||

sahajoliriyaṃ proktā śraddheyā yoghibhiḥ sadā |
ayaṃ śubhakaro yogho bhogha-yukto|api muktidaḥ || 94 ||

This is called Sahajolî, and should be relied on by Yogîs. It does good and gives mokṣa. 92.

अयं योगः पुण्यवतां धीराणां तत्त्व-दर्शिनाम |
निर्मत्सराणां वै सिध्येन्न तु मत्सर-शालिनाम || ९५ ||

ayaṃ yoghaḥ puṇyavatāṃ dhīrāṇāṃ tattva-darśinām |
nirmatsarāṇāṃ vai sidhyenna tu matsara-śālinām || 95 ||

This Yoga is achieved by courageous wise men, who are free from sloth, and cannot he accomplished by the slothful. 93.

The Amarolî.

अथ अमरोली
पित्तोल्बणत्वात्प्रथमाम्बु-धारां
विहाय निःसारतयान्त्यधाराम |
निष्हेव्यते शीतल-मध्य-धारा
कापालिके खण्डमते|अमरोली || ९६ ||

atha amarolī
pittolbaṇatvātprathamāmbu-dhārāṃ
vihāya niḥsāratayāntyadhārām |
niṣhevyate śītala-madhya-dhārā
kāpālike khaṇḍamate|amarolī || 96 ||

In the doctrine of the sect of the Kapâlikas, the Amarolî is the drinking of the mid stream; leaving the 1st, as it is a mixture of too much bile and the last, which is useless. 94.

अमरीं यः पिबेन्नित्यं नस्यं कुर्वन्दिने दिने |
वज्रोलीमभ्यसेत्सम्यक्सामरोलीति कथ्यते || ९७ ||

amarīṃ yaḥ pibennityaṃ nasyaṃ kurvandine dine |
vajrolīmabhyasetsamyaksāmarolīti kathyate || 97 ||

He who drinks Amarî, snuffs it daily, and practices Vajrolî, is called practising Amarolî. 95.

अभ्यासान्निःसृतां छान्द्रीं विभूत्या सह मिश्रयेत |
धारयेदुत्तमाङ्गेष्हु दिव्य-दृष्टिटः परजायते || ९८ ||

abhyāsānnihṣṛtāṃ chāndrīṃ vibhūtyā saha miśrayet | dhārayeduttamāngghesḥu divya-dṛṣḥṭiḥ prajāyate || 98 ||

पुंसो बिन्दुं समाकुनछ्य सम्यगभ्यास-पाटवात |
यदि नारी रजो रक्ष्हेद्वज्रोल्या सापि योगिनी || ९९ ||

puṃso binduṃ samākuñchya samyaghabhyāsa-pāṭavāt | yadi nārī rajo rakṣhedvajrolyā sāpi yoghinī || 99 ||

The *bindu* discharged in the practice of Vajrolî should be mixed with ashes, and the rubbing it on the best parts of the body gives divine sight. 96.

तस्याः किंछिद्रजो नाशं न गछ्छति न संशयः |
तस्याः शरीरे नादश्छ बिन्दुतामेव गछ्छति || १०० ||

tasyāḥ kiṃchidrajo nāśaṃ na ghachchati na saṃśayaḥ | tasyāḥ śarīre nādaścha bindutāmeva ghachchati || 100 ||

स बिन्दुस्तद्रजश्छैव एकीभूय सवदेहगौ |
वज्रोल्य-अभ्यास-योगेन सर्व-सिद्धिं परयछ्छतः || १०१ ||

sa bindustadrajaśchaiva ekībhūya svadehaghau | vajroly-abhyāsa-yoghena sarva-siddhiṃ prayachchataḥ || 101 ||

रक्ष्हेदाकुनछनादूर्ध्वं या रजः सा हि योगिनी |
अतीतानागतं वेत्ति खेछरी छ भवेद्ध्रुवम || १०२ ||

rakṣhedākuñchanādūrdhvaṃ yā rajaḥ sā hi yoghinī | atītānāghataṃ vetti khecharī cha bhaveddhruvam || 102 ||

देह-सिद्धिं छ लभते वज्रोल्य-अभ्यास-योगतः |
अयं पुण्य-करो योगो भोगे भुक्ते|अपि मुक्तिदः || १०३ ||

deha-siddhiṃ cha labhate vajroly-abhyāsa-yoghataḥ | ayaṃ puṇya-karo yogho bhoghe bhukte|api muktidaḥ || 103 ||

The Śakti châlana.

अथ शक्ति-छालनम
कुटिलाङ्गी कुण्डलिनी भुजङ्गी शक्तिरीश्वरी |
कुण्डल्यरुन्धती छैते शब्दाः पर्याय-वाछकाः || १०४ ||

atha śakti-chālanam
kuṭilāngghī kuṇḍalinī bhujangghī śaktirīśvarī |
kuṇḍalyarundhatī chaite śabdāḥ paryāya-vāchakāḥ || 104 ||

Kutilângî (crooked-bodied), Kuṇḍalinî, Bhujangî (a she-serpent) Śakti, Iśhwarî, Kundalî, Arundhatî,—all these words are synonymous. 97.

उद्घाटयेत्कपाटं तु यथा कुंछिकया हठात |
कुण्डलिन्या तथा योगी मोक्ष्हद्वारं विभेदयेत || १०५ ||

udghāṭayetkapāṭaṃ tu yathā kuṃchikayā haṭhāt |
kuṇḍalinyā tathā yoghī mokṣhadvāraṃ vibhedayet || 105 ||

As a door is opened with a key, so the Yogî opens the door of mukti by opening Kuṇḍalinî by means of Haṭha Yoga. 98.

येन मार्गेण गन्तव्यं बरह्म-सथानं निरामयम |
मुखेनाछ्छाद्य तद्वारं परसुप्ता परमेश्वरी || १०६ ||

yena mārgheṇa ghantavyaṃ brahma-sthānaṃ nirāmayam |
mukhenāchchādya tadvāraṃ prasuptā parameśvarī || 106 ||

The Parameśwarî (Kuṇḍalinî) sleeps, covering the hole of the passage by which one can go to the seat of Brahma which is free from pains. 99.

Keeping the feet in Vajra-âsana (Padma-âsana), hold them firmly with the hands. The position of the bulb then will be near the ankle joint, where it should be pressed. 107.

कन्दोर्ध्वे कुण्डली शक्तिः सुप्ता मोक्ष्हाय योगिनाम |
बन्धनाय छ मूढानां यस्तां वेत्ति स योगवित || १०७ ||

kandordhve kuṇḍalī śaktiḥ suptā mokṣhāya yoghinām |
bandhanāya cha mūḍhānāṃ yastāṃ vetti sa yoghavit || 107 ||

Kuṇḍalî Sakti sleeps on the bulb, for the purpose of giving moksa to Yogîs and bondage to the ignorant. He who knows it, knows Yoga. 100.

कुण्डली कुटिलाकारा सर्पवत्परिकीर्तिता |
सा शक्तिश्छालिता येन स मुक्तो नात्र संशयः || १०८ ||

kuṇḍalī kuṭilākārā sarpavatparikīrtitā |
sā śaktiśchālitā yena sa mukto nātra saṃśayaḥ || 108 ||

Kuṇḍalî is of a bent shape, and has been described to be like a serpent. He who has moved that Śakti is no doubt Mukta (released from bondage). 101.

गङ्गा-यमुनयोर्मध्ये बाल-रण्डां तपस्विनीम |
बलात्कारेण गृह्णीयात्तद्विष्ह्णोः परमं पदम || १०९ ||

ghanggha-yamunayormadhye bāla-raṇḍāṃ tapasvinīm |
balātkāreṇa ghṛhṇīyāttadviṣhṇoḥ paramaṃ padam || 109 ||

Youngster Tapaswini (a she-ascetic), lying between the Ganges and the Yamunâ, (Idâ and Pingalâ) should be caught hold of by force, to get the highest position. 102.

इडा भगवती गङ्गा पिङ्गला यमुना नदी |
इडा-पिङ्गलयोर्मध्ये बालरण्डा छ कुण्डली || ११० ||

iḍā bhaghavatī ghangghā pingghalā yamunā nadī |
iḍā-pingghalayormadhye bālaraṇḍā cha kuṇḍalī || 110 ||

Idâ is called goddess Ganges, Pingalâ goddess Yamunâ. In the middle of the Idâ and the Pingalâ is the infant widow, Kuṇḍalî. 103.

पुछ्छे परगृह्य भुजङ्गीं सुप्तामुद्बोधयेछ्छ ताम |
निद्रां विहाय सा शक्तिरूर्ध्वमुत्तिष्ह्ठते हठात || १११ ||

puchche praghṛhya bhujangghīṃ suptāmudbodhayechcha tām |
nidrāṃ vihāya sā śaktirūrdhvamuttiṣhṭhate haṭhāt || 111 ||

This sleeping she-serpent should be awakened by catching hold of her tail. By the force of Haṭha, the Śakti leaves her sleep, and starts upwards. 104.

अवस्थिता छैव फणावती सा
परातश्छ सायं परहरार्ध-मात्रम |
परपूर्य सूर्यात्परिधान-युक्त्या
परगृह्य नित्यं परिछालनीया || ११२ ||

avasthitā chaiva phaṇāvatī sā prātaścha sāyaṃ praharārdha-mātram | prapūrya sūryātparidhāna-yuktyā praghṝhya nityaṃ parichālanīyā || 112 ||

This she-serpent is situated in Mûlâdhâr. She should be caught and moved daily, morning and evening, for ½ a prahar (1½ hours), by filling with air through Pingalâ by the Paridhana method. 105.

ऊर्ध्वं वितस्ति-मात्रं तु विस्तारं छतुरङ्गुलम |
मृदुलं धवलं परोक्तं वेष्हिटताम्बर-लक्ष्हणम || ११३ ||

ūrdhvaṃ vitasti-mātraṃ tu vistāraṃ chaturangghulam | mṝdulaṃ dhavalaṃ proktaṃ veṣhṭitāmbara-lakṣhaṇam || 113 ||

The bulb is above the anus, a vitasti (12 angulas) long, and measures 4 angulas (3 inches) in extent and is soft and white, and appears as if a folded cloth. 106.

सति वज्रासने पादौ कराभ्यां धारयेद्दृढम |
गुल्फ-देश-समीपे छ कन्दं तत्र परपीडयेत || ११४ ||

sati vajrāsane pādau karābhyāṃ dhārayeddṝḍham | ghulpha-deśa-samīpe cha kandaṃ tatra prapīḍayet || 114 ||

Keeping the feet in Vajra-âsana (Padma-âsana), hold them firmly with the hands. The position of the bulb then will be near the ankle joint, where it should be pressed. 107.

वज्रासने सथितो योगी छालयित्वा छ कुण्डलीम |
कुर्यादनन्तरं भस्त्रां कुण्डलीमाशु बोधयेत || ११५ ||

vajrāsane sthito yoghī chālayitvā cha kuṇḍalīm | kuryādanantaraṃ bhastrāṃ kuṇḍalīmāśu bodhayet || 115 ||

The Yogî, sitting with Vajra-âsana and having moved Kuṇḍalî, should perform Bhastrikâ to awaken the Kuṇḍalî soon. 108.

भानोराकुनछनं कुर्यात्कुण्डलीं छालयेत्ततः |
मृत्यु-वक्त्र-गतस्यापि तस्य मृत्यु-भयं कुतः || ११६ ||

bhānorākuñchanaṃ kuryātkuṇḍalīṃ chālayettataḥ | mṝtyu-vaktra-ghatasyāpi tasya mṝtyu-bhayaṃ kutaḥ || 116 ||

Bhânu (Sûrya, near the navel) should be contracted (by contracting the navel) which will move the Kuṇḍalî. There is no fear for him who does so, even if he has entered the mouth of death. 109.

मुहूर्त-दवय-पर्यन्तं निर्भयं छालनादसौ |
ऊर्ध्वमाकृष्ह्यते किंछित्सुष्हुम्णायां समुद्गता || ११७ ||

muhūrta-dvaya-paryantaṃ nirbhayaṃ chālanādasau |
ūrdhvamākṝṣhyate kiṃchitsuṣhumṇāyāṃ samudghatā || 117 ||

By moving this, for two muhûrtas, it is drawn up a little by entering the Suṣumnâ (spinal column). 110.

तेन कुण्डलिनी तस्याः सुष्हुम्णाया मुखं धरुवम |
जहाति तस्मात्प्राणो|अयं सुष्हुम्णां वरजति सवतः || ११८ ||

tena kuṇḍalinī tasyāḥ suṣhumṇāyā mukhaṃ dhruvam |
jahāti tasmatpraṇo|ayaṃ suṣhumṇaṃ vrajati svataḥ || 118 ||

By this Kuṇḍalinî leaves the entrance of the Suṣumnâ at once, and the Prâṇa enters it of itself. 111.

तस्मात्संछालयेन्नित्यं सुख-सुप्तामरुन्धतीम |
तस्याः संछालनेनैव योगी रोगैः परमुछ्यते || ११९ ||

tasmātsaṃchālayennityaṃ sukha-suptāmarundhatīm |
tasyāḥ saṃchālanenaiva yoghī roghaiḥ pramuchyate || 119 ||

Therefore, this comfortably sleeping Arundhatî should always be moved; for by so doing the Yogî gets rid of diseases. 112.

येन संछालिता शक्तिः स योगी सिद्धि-भाजनम |
किमत्र बहुनोक्तेन कालं जयति लीलया || १२० ||

yena saṃchālitā śaktiḥ sa yoghī siddhi-bhājanam |
kimatra bahunoktena kālaṃ jayati līlayā || 120 ||

The Yogî, who has been able to move the Śakti deserves success. It is useless to say more, suffice it to say that he conquers death playfully. 113.

बरह्मछर्य-रतस्यैव नित्यं हित-मिताशिनः |
मण्डलाद्दृश्यते सिद्धिः कुण्डल्य-अभ्यास-योगिनः || १२१ ||

brahmacharya-ratasyaiva nityaṃ hita-mitāśinaḥ |
maṇḍalāddṝśyate siddhiḥ kuṇḍaly-abhyāsa-yoghinaḥ || 121 ||

The Yogî observing Brahmacharya (continence and always eating sparingly, gets success within 40 days by practice with the Kuṇḍalinî. 114.

कुण्डलीं छालयित्वा तु भस्त्रां कुर्याद्विशेष्हतः |
एवमभ्यस्यतो नित्यं यमिनो यम-भीः कुतः || १२२ ||

kuṇḍalīṃ chālayitvā tu bhastrāṃ kuryādviśeṣhataḥ |
evamabhyasyato nityaṃ yamino yama-bhīḥ kutaḥ || 122 ||

After moving the Kuṇḍalî, plenty of Bhastrâ should be performed. By such practice, he has no fear from the god of death. 115.

दवा-सप्तति-सहस्राणां नाडीनां मल-शोधने |
कुतः परक्ष्हालनोपायः कुण्डल्य-अभ्यसनादृते || १२३ ||

dvā-saptati-sahasrāṇāṃ nāḍīnāṃ mala-śodhane |
kutaḥ prakṣhālanopāyaḥ kuṇḍaly-abhyasanādṝte || 123 ||

There is no other way, but the practice of the Kuṇḍalî, for washing away the impurities of 72,000 Nâdîs. 116.

इयं तु मध्यमा नाडी दृढाभ्यासेन योगिनाम |
आसन-पराण-संयाम-मुद्राभिः सरला भवेत || १२४ ||

iyaṃ tu madhyamā nāḍī dṝḍhābhyāsena yoghinām |
āsana-prāṇa-saṃyāma-mudrābhiḥ saralā bhavet || 124 ||

This middle Nâdî becomes straight by steady practice of postures; Prâṇâyâma and Mudrâs of Yogîs. 117.

अभ्यासे तु विनिद्राणां मनो धृत्वा समाधिना |
रुद्राणी वा परा मुद्रा भद्रां सिद्धिं परयछ्छति || १२५ ||

abhyāse tu vinidrāṇāṃ mano dhṝtvā samādhinā |
rudrāṇī vā parā mudrā bhadrāṃ siddhiṃ prayachchati || 125 ||

Those whose sleep has decreased by practice and mind has become calm by samâdhi, get beneficial accomplishments by Sâmbhavî and other Mudrâs. 118.

राज-योगं विना पृथ्वी राज-योगं विना निशा |
राज-योगं विना मुद्रा विछित्रापि न शोभते || १२६ ||

rāja-yoghaṃ vinā pṛthvī rāja-yoghaṃ vinā niśā | rāja-yoghaṃ vinā mudrā vichitrāpi na śobhate || 126 ||

Without Raja Yoga, this earth, the night, and the Mudrâs, be they howsoever wonderful, do not appear beautiful. 119.

Note.—Raja Yoga = âsana. Earth = steadiness, calmness. Night = Kumbhaka; cessations of the activity of the Prâṇa, just as King's officials cease moving at night. Hence night means absence of motion, *i.e.*, Kumbhaka.

मारुतस्य विधिं सर्वं मनो-युक्तं समभ्यसेत |
इतरत्र न कर्तव्या मनो-वृत्तिर्मनीष्हिणा || १२७ ||

mārutasya vidhiṃ sarvaṃ mano-yuktaṃ samabhyaset | itaratra na kartavyā mano-vṛttirmanīṣhiṇā || 127 ||

All the practices relating to the air should be performed with concentrated mind. A wise man should not allow his mind to wander away. 120.

इति मुद्रा दश परोक्ता आदिनाथेन शम्भुना |
एकैका तासु यमिनां महा-सिद्धि-परदायिनी || १२८ ||

iti mudrā daśa proktā ādināthena śambhunā | ekaikā tāsu yamināṃ mahā-siddhi-pradāyinī || 128 ||

These are the Mudrâs, as explained by Âdinâtha (Śiva). Every one of them is the giver of great accomplishments to the practiser. 121.

उपदेशं हि मुद्राणां यो दत्ते साम्प्रदायिकम |
स एव शरी-गुरुः सवामी साक्ष्हादीश्वर एव सः || १२९ ||

upadeśaṃ hi mudrāṇāṃ yo datte sāmpradāyikam | sa eva śrī-ghuruḥ svāmī sākṣhādīśvara eva saḥ || 129 ||

He is really the *guru* and to be considered as Îśvara in human form who teaches the Mudrâs as handed down from guru to guru. 122.

तस्य वाक्य-परो भूत्वा मुद्राभ्यासे समाहितः | अणिमादि-गुणैः सार्धं लभते काल-वञ्छनम || १३० ||

tasya vākya-paro bhūtvā mudrābhyāse samāhitaḥ | aṇimādi-ghuṇaiḥ sārdhaṃ labhate kāla-vañchanam || 130 ||

Engaging in practice, by putting faith in his words, one gets the Siddhis of Anima, etc., as also evades death. 123.

End of chapter III, on the Exposition of the Mudrâs.

इति हठ-परदीपिकायां तृतीयोपदेशः |

iti haṭha-pradīpikāyāṃ tṛtīyopadeśaḥ |

CHAPTER IV.

On Samâdhi.

|| ४ || छतुर्थोपदेशः

|| 4 || chaturthopadeśaḥ

नमः शिवाय गुरवे नाद-बिन्दु-कलात्मने | निरञ्जन-पदं याति नित्यं तत्र परायणः || १ ||

namaḥ śivāya ghurave nāda-bindu-kalātmane | nirañjana-padaṃ yāti nityaṃ tatra parāyaṇaḥ || 1 ||

Salutation to the Gurû, the dispenser of happiness to all, appearing as Nâda, Vindû and Kalâ. One who is devoted to Him, obtains the highest bliss. 1.

अथेदानीं परवक्ष्ह्यामि समाधिक्रममुत्तमम | मृत्युघ्नं छ सुखोपायं बरह्मानन्द-करं परम || २ ||

athedānīṃ pravakṣhyāmi samādhikramamuttamam | mṝtyughnaṃ cha sukhopāyaṃ brahmānanda-karaṃ param || 2 ||

Now I will describe a regular method of attaining to Samâdhi, which destroys death, is the means for obtaining happiness, and gives the Brahmânanda. 2.

राज-योगः समाधिश्छ उन्मनी छ मनोन्मनी | अमरत्वं लयस्तत्त्वं शून्याशून्यं परं पदम || ३ || अमनस्कं तथाद्वैतं निरालम्बं निरञ्जनम | जीवन्मुक्तिश्छ सहजा तुर्या छेत्येक-वाछकाः || ४ ||

rāja-yoghaḥ samādhiścha unmanī cha manonmanī | amaratvaṃ layastattvaṃ śūnyāśūnyaṃ paraṃ padam || 3 ||

amanaskaṃ tathādvaitaṃ nirālambaṃ nirañjanam | jīvanmuktiścha sahajā turyā chetyeka-vāchakāḥ || 4 ||

Raja Yogî, Samâdhi, Unmani, Mauonmanî, Amarativa, Laya, Tatwa, Sûnya, Aśûnya, Parama Pada, Amanaska, Adwaitama, Nirãlamba, Nirañjana, Jîwana Mukti, Sahajâ, Turyâ, are all synonymous. 3-4.

सलिले सैन्धवं यद्वत्साम्यं भजति योगतः | तथात्म-मनसोरैक्यं समाधिरभिधीयते || ५ ||

salile saindhavaṃ yadvatsāmyaṃ bhajati yoghataḥ | tathātma-manasoraikyaṃ samādhirabhidhīyate || 5 ||

As salt being dissolved in water becomes one with it, so when Âtmâ and mind become one, it is called Samâdhi. 5.

यदा संक्ष्हीयते पराणो मानसं छ परलीयते | तदा समरसत्वं छ समाधिरभिधीयते || ६ ||

yadā saṃkṣhīyate prāṇo mānasaṃ cha pralīyate | tadā samarasatvaṃ cha samādhirabhidhīyate || 6 ||

When the Prâṇa becomes lean (vigourless) and the mind becomes absorbed, then their becoming equal is called Samâdhi. 6.

तत-समं छ दवयोरैक्यं जीवात्म-परमात्मनोः | परनष्ह्ट-सर्व-सङ्कल्पः समाधिः सो|अभिधीयते || ७ ||

tat-samaṃ cha dvayoraikyaṃ jīvātma-paramātmanoḥ | pranaṣhṭa-sarva-sangkalpaḥ samādhiḥ so|abhidhīyate || 7 ||

This equality and oneness of the self and the ultra self, when all Saṃkalpas cease to exist, is called Samâdhi. 7.

राज-योगस्य माहात्म्यं को वा जानाति तत्त्वतः | जज्ञानं मुक्तिः सथितिः सिद्धिर्गुरु-वाक्येन लभ्यते || ८ ||

rāja-yoghasya māhātmyaṃ ko vā jānāti tattvataḥ | jñānaṃ muktiḥ sthitiḥ siddhirghuru-vākyena labhyate || 8 ||

Or, who can know the true greatness of the Raja Yoga. Knowledge, mukti, condition, and Siddhîs can be learnt by instructions from a *gurû* alone. 8.

दुर्लभो विष्हय-तयागो दुर्लभं तत्त्व-दर्शनम |
दुर्लभा सहजावस्था सद-गुरोः करुणां विना || ९ ||

durlabho viṣhaya-tyāgho durlabhaṃ tattva-darśanam |
durlabhā sahajāvasthā sad-ghuroḥ karuṇāṃ vinā || 9 ||

Indifference to worldly enjoyments is very difficult to obtain, and equally difficult is the knowledge of the Realities to obtain. It is very difficult to get the condition of Samâdhi, without the favour of a true *guru*. 9.

विविधैरासनैः कुभैर्विछित्रैः करणैरपि |
परबुद्धायां महा-शक्तौ पराणः शून्ये परलीयते || १० ||

vividhairāsanaiḥ kubhairvichitraiḥ karaṇairapi |
prabuddhāyāṃ mahā-śaktau prāṇaḥ śūnye pralīyate || 10 ||

By means of various postures and different Kumbhakas, when the great power (Kuṇḍalî) awakens, then the Prâṇa becomes absorbed in Sûnya (Samâdhi). 10.

उत्पन्न-शक्ति-बोधस्य तयक्त-निःशेष्ह-कर्मणः |
योगिनः सहजावस्था सवयमेव परजायते || ११ ||

utpanna-śakti-bodhasya tyakta-niḥśeṣha-karmaṇaḥ |
yoghinaḥ sahajāvasthā svayameva prajāyate || 11 ||

The Yogî whose śakti has awakened, and who has renounced all actions, attains to the condition of Samâdhi, without any effort. 11.

सुष्हुम्णा-वाहिनि पराणे शून्ये विशति मानसे |
तदा सर्वाणि कर्माणि निर्मूलयति योगवित || १२ ||

suṣhumṇā-vāhini prāṇe śūnye viśati mānase |
tadā sarvāṇi karmāṇi nirmūlayati yoghavit || 12 ||

When the Prâṇa flows in the Suṣumnâ, and the mind has entered śûnya, then the Yogî is free from the effects of Karmas. 12.

अमराय नमस्तुभ्यं सो|अपि कालस्त्वया जितः | पतितं वदने यस्य जगदेतच्छराछरम || १३ ||

amarāya namastubhyaṃ so|api kālastvayā jitaḥ | patitaṃ vadane yasya jaghadetachcharācharam || 13 ||

O Immortal one (that is, the yogi who has attained to the condition of Samâdhi), I salute thee! Even death itself, into whose mouth the whole of this movable and immovable world has fallen, has been conquered by thee. 13.

छित्ते समत्वमापन्ने वायौ वरजति मध्यमे | तदामरोली वज्रोली सहजोली परजायते || १४ ||

chitte samatvamāpanne vāyau vrajati madhyame | tadāmarolī vajrolī sahajolī prajāyate || 14 ||

Amarolî, Vajrolî and Sahajolî are accomplished when the mind becomes calm and Prâṇa has entered the middle channel. 14.

जञानं कुतो मनसि सम्भवतीह तावत पराणो|अपि जीवति मनो मरियते न यावत | पराणो मनो दवयमिदं विलयं नयेद्यो मोक्ष्हं स गच्छति नरो न कथंछिदन्यः || १५ ||

jñānaṃ kuto manasi sambhavatīha tāvat prāṇo|api jīvati mano mriyate na yāvat | prāṇo mano dvayamidaṃ vilayaṃ nayedyo mokṣhaṃ sa ghachchati naro na kathaṃchidanyaḥ || 15 ||

How can it he possible to get knowledge, so long as the Prâṇa is living and the mind has not died? No one else can get mokṣa, except one who can make one's Prâṇa and mind latent. 15.

जञात्वा सुष्हुम्णासद-भेदं कृत्वा वायुं छ मध्यगम | सथित्वा सदैव सुस्थाने बरह्म-रन्ध्रे निरोधयेत || १६ ||

jñātvā suṣhumṇāsad-bhedaṃ kṛtvā vāyuṃ cha madhyagham | sthitvā sadaiva susthāne brahma-randhre nirodhayet || 16 ||

Always living in a good locality and having known the secret of the Suṣumnâ, which has a middle course, and making the Vâyu move in it., (the Yogî) should restrain the Vâyu in the Brahma randhra. 16.

सूर्य-छन्द्रमसौ धत्तः कालं रात्रिन्दिवात्मकम |
भोक्त्री सुष्हुम्ना कालस्य गुह्यमेतदुदाहृतम || १७ ||

sūrya-chandramasau dhattaḥ kālaṃ rātrindivātmakam |
bhoktrī suṣhumnā kālasya ghuhyametadudāhṛtam || 17 ||

Time, in the form of night and day, is made by the sun and the moon. That, the Suṣumnâ devours this time (death) even, is a great secret. 17.

दवा-सप्तति-सहस्राणि नाडी-दवाराणि पञ्जरे |
सुष्हुम्णा शाम्भवी शक्तिः शेष्हास्त्वेव निरर्थकाः || १८ ||

dvā-saptati-sahasrāṇi nāḍī-dvārāṇi pañjare |
suṣhumṇā śāmbhavī śaktiḥ śeṣhāstveva nirarthakāḥ || 18 ||

In this body there are 72,000 openings of Nâdis; of these, the Suṣumnâ, which has the Śâmhhavî Sakti in it, is the only important one, the rest are useless. 18.

वायुः परिछितो यस्मादग्निना सह कुण्डलीम |
बोधयित्वा सुष्हुम्णायां परविशेदनिरोधतः || १९ ||

vāyuḥ parichito yasmādaghninā saha kuṇḍalīm |
bodhayitvā suṣhumṇāyāṃ praviśedanirodhataḥ || 19 ||

The Vâyu should be made to enter the Suṣumnâ without restraint by him who has practised the control of breathing and has awakened the Kuṇḍali by the (gastric) fire. `19

सुष्हुम्णा-वाहिनि पराणे सिद्ध्यत्येव मनोन्मनी |
अन्यथा तवितराभ्यासाः परयासायैव योगिनाम || २० ||

suṣhumṇā-vāhini prāṇe siddhyatyeva manonmanī |
anyathā tvitarābhyāsāḥ prayāsāyaiva yoghinām || 20 ||

The Prâṇa, flowing through the Suṣumnâ, brings about the condition of manonmaṇî; other practices are simply futile for the Yogî. 20.

पवनो बध्यते येन मनस्तेनैव बध्यते ।
मनश्छ बध्यते येन पवनस्तेन बध्यते || २१ ||

pavano badhyate yena manastenaiva badhyate |
manaścha badhyate yena pavanastena badhyate || 21 ||

By whom the breathing has been controlled, by him the activities of the mind also have been controlled; and, conversely, by whom the activities of the mind have been controlled, by him the breathing also has been controlled. 21.

हेतु-दवयं तु छित्तस्य वासना छ समीरणः ।
तयोर्विनष्ह्ट एकस्मिन्तौ दवावपि विनश्यतः || २२ ||

hetu-dvayaṃ tu chittasya vāsanā cha samīraṇaḥ |
tayorvinaṣhṭa ekasmintau dvāvapi vinaśyataḥ || 22 ||

There are two causes of the activities of the mind: (1) Vâsanâ (desires) and (2) the respiration (the Prâṇa). Of these, the destruction of the one is the destruction of both. 22.

मनो यत्र विलीयेत पवनस्तत्र लीयते ।
पवनो लीयते यत्र मनस्तत्र विलीयते || २३ ||

mano yatra vilīyeta pavanastatra līyate |
pavano līyate yatra manastatra vilīyate || 23 ||

Breathing is lessened when the mind becomes absorbed, and the mind becomes absorbed when the Prâṇa is restrained. 23.

दुग्धाम्बुवत्संमिलितावुभौ तौ
तुल्य-करियौ मानस-मारुतौ हि ।
यतो मरुत्तत्र मनः-परवृत्तिर
यतो मनस्तत्र मरुत-परवृत्तिः || २४ ||

dughdhāmbuvatsaṃmilitāvubhau tau
tulya-kriyau mānasa-mārutau hi |
yato maruttatra manaḥ-pravṛttir
yato manastatra marut-pravṛttiḥ || 24 ||

Both the mind and the breath are united together, like milk and water; and both of them are equal in their activities. Mind begins its activities where there is the breath, and the Parana begins its activities where there is the mind. 24.

तत्रैक-नाशादपरस्य नाश
एक-परवृत्तेरपर-परवृत्तिः ।
अध्वस्तयोश्छेन्द्रिय-वर्ग-वृत्तिः
परध्वस्तयोर्मोक्षह-पदस्य सिद्धिः ॥ २५ ॥

tatraika-nāśādaparasya nāśa
eka-pravṝtterapara-pravṝttiḥ |
adhvastayośchendriya-vargha-vṝttiḥ
pradhvastayormokṣha-padasya siddhiḥ || 25 ||

By the suspension of the one, therefore, comes the suspension of the other, and by the operations of the one are brought about the operations of the other. When they are present, the Indriyas (the senses) remain engaged in their proper functions, and when they become latent then there is moksa. 25.

रसस्य मनसश्छैव छञ्छलत्वं सवभावतः ।
रसो बद्धो मनो बद्धं किं न सिद्ध्यति भूतले ॥ २६ ॥

rasasya manasaśchaiva chañchalatvaṃ svabhāvataḥ |
raso baddho mano baddhaṃ kiṃ na siddhyati bhūtale || 26 ||

By nature, Mercury and mind are unsteady: there is nothing in the world which cannot be accomplished when these are made steady. 26.

मूर्छ्छितो हरते वयाधीन्मृतो जीवयति सवयम ।
बद्धः खेछरतां धत्ते रसो वायुश्छ पार्वति ॥ २७ ॥

mūrchchito harate vyādhīnmṝto jīvayati svayam |
baddhaḥ khecharatāṃ dhatte raso vāyuścha pārvati || 27 ||

O Pârvati! Mercury and breathing, when made steady, destroy diseases and the dead himself comes to life (by their means). By their (proper) control, moving in the air is attained. 27.

मनः सथैर्यं सथिरो वायुस्ततो बिन्दुः सथिरो भवेत ।
बिन्दु-सथैर्यात्सदा सत्त्वं पिण्ड-सथैर्यं परजायते ॥ २८ ॥

manaḥ sthairyaṃ sthiro vāyustato binduḥ sthiro bhavet |
bindu-sthairyātsadā sattvaṃ piṇḍa-sthairyaṃ prajāyate || 28 ||

The breathing is calmed when the mind becomes steady and calm; and hence the preservation of *bindu*. The preservation of this latter makes the satwa established in the body. 28.

इन्द्रियाणां मनो नाथो मनोनाथस्तु मारुतः |
मारुतस्य लयो नाथः स लयो नादमाश्रितः || २९ ||

indriyāṇāṃ mano nātho manonāthastu mārutaḥ |
mārutasya layo nāthaḥ sa layo nādamāśritaḥ || 29 ||

Mind is the master of the senses, and the breath is the master of the mind. The breath in its turn is subordinate to the laya (absorption), and that laya depends on the nâda. 29.

सो|अयमेवास्तु मोक्ष्हाख्यो मास्तु वापि मतान्तरे |
मनः-पराण-लये कश्छिदानन्दः सम्प्रवर्तते || ३० ||

so|ayamevāstu mokṣhākhyo māstu vāpi matāntare |
manaḥ-prāṇa-laye kaśchidānandaḥ sampravartate || 30 ||

This very laya is what is called mokṣa, or, being a sectarian, you may not call it mokṣa; but when the mind becomes absorbed, a sort of ecstacy is experienced. 30.

परनष्ह्ट-शवास-निश्वासः परध्वस्त-विष्हय-गरहः |
निश्छेष्ह्टो निर्विकारश्छ लयो जयति योगिनाम || ३१ ||

pranaṣhṭa-śvāsa-niśvāsaḥ pradhvasta-viṣhaya-ghrahaḥ |
niścheṣhṭo nirvikāraścha layo jayati yoghinām || 31 ||

By the suspension of respiration and the annihilation of the enjoyments of the senses, when the mind becomes devoid of all the activities and remains changeless, then the Yogî attains to the Laya Stage. 31.

उछ्छिन्न-सर्व-सङ्कल्पो निःशेष्हाशेष्ह-छेष्ह्टितः |
सवावगम्यो लयः को|अपि जायते वाग-अगोछरः || ३२ ||

uchchinna-sarva-sangkalpo niḥśeṣhāśeṣha-cheṣhṭitaḥ |
svāvaghamyo layaḥ ko|api jāyate vāgh-aghocharaḥ || 32 ||

When all the thoughts and activities are destroyed, then the Laya Stage is produced, to describe which is beyond the power of speech, being known by self-experience alone. 32.

यत्र दृष्टिर्लयस्तत्र भूतेन्द्रिय-सनातनी ।
सा शक्तिर्जीव-भूतानां दवे अलक्ष्ह्ये लयं गते || ३३ ||

yatra dṛṣhṭirlayastatra bhūtendriya-sanātanī |
sā śaktirjīva-bhūtānāṃ dve alakṣhye layaṃ ghate || 33 ||

They often speak of Laya, Laya; but what is meant by it?

लयो लय इति पराहुः कीदृशं लय-लक्ष्हणम ।
अपुनर-वासनोत्थानाल्लयो विष्हय-विस्मृतिः || ३४ ||

layo laya iti prāhuḥ kīdṛśaṃ laya-lakṣhaṇam |
apunar-vāsanotthānāllayo viṣhaya-vismṛtiḥ || 34 ||

Laya is simply then forgetting of the objects of senses when the Vâsanâs (desires) do not rise into existence again. 33.

The Sâmbhavî Mudrâ.

वेद-शास्त्र-पुराणानि सामान्य-गणिका इव ।
एकैव शाम्भवी मुद्रा गुप्ता कुल-वधूरिव || ३५ ||

veda-śāstra-purāṇāni sāmānya-ghaṇikā iva |
ekaiva śāmbhavī mudrā ghuptā kula-vadhūriva || 35 ||

The Vedas and the Śâstras are like ordinary public women. Śâmhhavî Mudrâ is the one, which is secluded like a respectable lady. 34.

अथ शाम्भवी
अन्तर्लक्ष्हयं बहिर्दृष्हिटर्निमेष्होन्मेष्ह-वर्जिता ।
एष्हा सा शाम्भवी मुद्रा वेद-शास्त्रेष्हु गोपिता || ३६ ||

atha śāmbhavī
antarlakṣhyaṃ bahirdṛṣhṭirnimeṣhonmeṣha-varjitā |
eṣhā sā śāmbhavī mudrā veda-śāstreṣhu ghopitā || 36 ||

Aiming at Brahman inwardly, while keeping the sight directed to the external objects, without blinking the eyes, is called the Sâmbhavî Mudrâ, hidden in the Vedas and the Sâstras. 35.

अन्तर्लक्ष्ह्य-विलीन-छित्त-पवनो योगी यदा वर्तते दृष्ह्ट्या निश्छल-तारया बहिरधः पश्यन्नपश्यन्नपि | मुद्रेयं खलु शाम्भवी भवति सा लब्धा परसादाद्गुरोः शून्याशून्य-विलक्ष्हणं सफुरति तत्तत्त्वं पदं शाम्भवम || ३७ ||

antarlakṣhya-vilīna-chitta-pavano yoghī yadā vartate dṛṣhṭyā niśchala-tārayā bahiradhaḥ paśyannapaśyannapi | mudreyaṃ khalu śāmbhavī bhavati sā labdhā prasādādghuroḥ śūnyāśūnya-vilakṣhaṇaṃ sphurati tattattvaṃ padaṃ śāmbhavam || 37 ||

When the Yogî remains inwardly attentive to the Brahman, keeping the mind and the Prâṇa absorbed, and the sight steady, as if seeing everything while in reality seeing nothing outside, below, or above, verily then it is called the Sâmbhavî Mudrâ, which is learnt by the favour of a *guru*. Whatever, wonderful, Sûnya or Asûnya is perceived, is to be regarded as the manifestation of that great Śambhû (Śiva.) 36.

शरी-शाम्भव्याश्छ खेछर्या अवस्था-धाम-भेदतः | भवेछ्छित्त-लयानन्दः शून्ये छित-सुख-रूपिणि || ३८ ||

śrī-śāmbhavyāścha khecharyā avasthā-dhāma-bhedataḥ | bhavechchitta-layānandaḥ śūnye chit-sukha-rūpiṇi || 38 ||

The two states, the Sâmbhavî and the Khecharî, are different because of their seats (being the heart and the space between the eyebrows respectively); but both cause happiness, for the mind becomes absorbed in the Chita-sukha-Rupa-âtmana which is void. 37.

The Unmanî.

तारे जयोतिष्हि संयोज्य किंछिदुन्नमयेद्भ्रुवौ | पूर्व-योगं मनो युनजन्नुन्मनी-कारकः कष्हणात || ३९ ||

tāre jyotiṣhi saṃyojya kiṃchidunnamayedbhruvau | pūrva-yoghaṃ mano yuñjannunmanī-kārakaḥ kṣhaṇāt || 39 ||

Fix the gaze on the light (seen on the tip of the nose) and raise the eyebrows a little, with the mind contemplating as before (in the Śambhavî Mudrâ, that is, inwardly thinking of Brahma, but apparently looking outside.) This will create the Unmanî avasthâ at once. 38.

The Târaka.

केछिदागम-जालेन केछिन्निगम-सङ्कुलैः ।
केछित्तर्केण मुह्यन्ति नैव जानन्ति तारकम || ४० ||

kechidāghama-jālena kechinnighama-sangkulaiḥ ।
kechittarkeṇa muhyanti naiva jānanti tārakam || 40 ||

Some are devoted to the Vedas, some to Nigama, while others are enwrapt in Logic, but none knows the value of this mudrâ, which enables one to cross the ocean of existence 39.

अर्धोन्मीलित-लोछनः सथिर-मना नासाग्र-दत्तेक्ष्हणश
छन्द्रार्कावपि लीनतामुपनयन्निस्पन्द-भावेन यः ।
जयोती-रूपमशेष्ह-बीजमखिलं देदीप्यमानं परं
तत्त्वं तत-पदमेति वस्तु परमं वाछ्यं किमत्राधिकम || ४१ ||

ardhonmīlita-lochanaḥ sthira-manā nāsāghra-dattekṣhaṇaś
chandrārkāvapi līnatāmupanayannispanda-bhāvena yaḥ ।
jyotī-rūpamaśeṣha-bījamakhilaṃ dedīpyamānaṃ paraṃ
tattvaṃ tat-padameti vastu paramaṃ vāchyaṃ kimatrādhikam || 41 ||

With steady calm mind and half closed eyes, fixed on the tip of the nose, stopping the Idâ and the Pingalâ without blinking, he who can see the light which is the all, the seed, the entire brilliant, great Tatwama, approaches Him, who is the great object. What is the use of more talk? 40.

दिवा न पूजयेल्लिङ्गं रात्रौ छैव न पूजयेत ।
सर्वदा पूजयेल्लिङ्गं दिवारात्रि-निरोधतः || ४२ ||

divā na pūjayellingghaṃ rātrau chaiva na pūjayet ।
sarvadā pūjayellingghaṃ divārātri-nirodhataḥ || 42 ||

One should not meditate on the Linga (*i.e.*, Âtman) in the day (*i.e.*, while Sûrya or Pingalâ is working) or at night (when Idâ is working), but should always contemplate after restraining both. 41.

The Khecharî.

अथ खेछरी
सव्य-दक्षिहण-नाडी-सथो मध्ये छरति मारुतः |
तिष्हठते खेछरी मुद्रा तस्मिन्स्थाने न संशयः || ४३ ||

atha khecharī
savya-dakṣhiṇa-nāḍī-stho madhye charati mārutaḥ |
tiṣhṭhate khecharī mudrā tasminsthāne na saṃśayaḥ || 43 ||

When the air has ceased to move in the right and the left nostrils, and has begun to flow in the middle path, then the Khecharî Mudrâ, can be accomplished there. There is no doubt of this. 42.

इडा-पिङ्गलयोर्मध्ये शून्यं छैवानिलं गरसेत |
तिष्हठते खेछरी मुद्रा तत्र सत्यं पुनः पुनः || ४४ ||

iḍā-pingghalayormadhye śūnyaṃ chaivānilaṃ ghraset |
tiṣhṭhate khecharī mudrā tatra satyaṃ punaḥ punaḥ || 44 ||

If the Prâṇa can he drawn into the Sûnya (Suṣumnâ), which is between the Idâ and the Pingalâ, and male motionless there, then the Khecharî Mudrâ can truly become steady there. 43.

सूर्च्याछन्द्रमसोर्मध्ये निरालम्बान्तरे पुनः |
संस्थिता वयोम-छक्रे या सा मुद्रा नाम खेछरी || ४५ ||

sūrchyāchandramasormadhye nirālambāntare punaḥ |
saṃsthitā vyoma-chakre yā sā mudrā nāma khecharī || 45 ||

That Mudrâ is called Khecharî which is performed in the supportless space between the Sûrya and the Chandra (the Idâ and the Pingalâ) and called the Vyoma Chakra. 44.

सोमाद्यत्रोदिता धारा साक्षात्सा शिव-वल्लभा |
पूरयेदतुलां दिव्यां सुष्हुम्णां पश्छिमे मुखे || ४६ ||

somādyatroditā dhārā sākṣhātsā śiva-vallabhā |
pūrayedatulāṃ divyāṃ suṣhumṇāṃ paśchime mukhe || 46 ||

The Khecharî which causes the stream to flow from the Chandra (Śoma) is beloved of Śiva. The incomparable divine Suṣumnâ should be closed by the tongue drawn back. 45.

पुरस्ताच्छचैव पूर्येत निश्छिता खेछरी भवेत |
अभ्यस्ता खेछरी मुद्राप्युन्मनी सम्प्रजायते || ४७ ||

purastāchchaiva pūryeta niśchitā khecharī bhavet |
abhyastā khecharī mudrāpyunmanī samprajāyate || 47 ||

It can be closed from the front also (by stopping the movements of the Prâṇa), and then surely it becomes the Khecharî. By practice, this Khecharî leads to Unmanî. 46.

भरुवोर्मध्ये शिव-सथानं मनस्तत्र विलीयते |
जञातव्यं तत-पदं तुर्यं तत्र कालो न विद्यते || ४८ ||

bhruvormadhye śiva-sthānaṃ manastatra vilīyate |
jñātavyaṃ tat-padaṃ turyaṃ tatra kālo na vidyate || 48 ||

The seat of Śiva is between the eyebrows, and the mind becomes absorbed there. This condition (in which the mind is thus absorbed) is known as Tûrya, and death has no access there. 47.

अभ्यसेत्खेछरीं तावद्यावत्स्याद्योग-निद्रितः |
सम्प्राप्त-योग-निद्रस्य कालो नास्ति कदाछन || ४९ ||

abhyasetkhecharīṃ tāvadyāvatsyādyogha-nidritaḥ |
samprāpta-yogha-nidrasya kālo nāsti kadāchana || 49 ||

The Khecharî should be practised till there is Yoga-nidrâ (Samâdhi). One who has induced Yoga-nidrâ, cannot fall a victim to death. 48.

निरालम्बं मनः कृत्वा न किंछिदपि छिन्तयेत |
स-बाह्याभ्यन्तरं वयोम्नि घटवत्तिष्ठति धरुवम || ५० ||

nirālambaṃ manaḥ kṛtvā na kiṃchidapi chintayet |
sa-bāhyābhyantaraṃ vyomni ghaṭavattiṣhṭhati dhruvam || 50 ||

Freeing the mind from all thoughts and thinking of nothing, one should sit firmly like a pot in the space (surrounded and filled with the ether). 49.

बाह्य-वायुर्यथा लीनस्तथा मध्यो न संशयः |
सव-सथाने सथिरतामेति पवनो मनसा सह || ५१ ||

bāhya-vāyuryathā līnastathā madhyo na saṃśayaḥ |
sva-sthāne sthiratāmeti pavano manasā saha || 51 ||

As the air, in and out of the body, remains unmoved, so the breath with mind becomes steady in its place (*i.e.*, in Brahma randhra). 50.

एवमभ्यस्यतस्तस्य वायु-मार्गे दिवानिशम |
अभ्यासाज्जीर्यते वायुर्मनस्तत्रैव लीयते || ५२ ||

evamabhyasyatastasya vāyu-mārghe divāniśam |
abhyāsājjīryate vāyurmanastatraiva līyate || 52 ||

By thus practising, night and day, the breathing is brought under control, and, as the practice increases, the mind becomes calm and steady. 51.

अमृतैः पलावयेद्देहमापाद-तल-मस्तकम |
सिद्ध्यत्येव महा-कायो महा-बल-पराक्रमः || ५३ ||

amṛtaiḥ plāvayeddehamāpāda-tala-mastakam |
siddhyatyeva mahā-kāyo mahā-bala-parākramaḥ || 53 ||

By rubbing the body over with Amrita (exuding from the moon), from head to foot, one gets Mahâkâyâ, *i.e.*, great strength and energy. 52.

End of the Khecharî.

शक्ति-मध्ये मनः कृत्वा शक्तिं मानस-मध्यगाम |
मनसा मन आलोक्य धारयेत्परमं पदम || ५४ ||

śakti-madhye manaḥ kṛtvā śaktiṃ mānasa-madhyaghām |
manasā mana ālokya dhārayetparamaṃ padam || 54 ||

Placing the mind into the Kuṇḍalini, and getting the latter into the mind, by looking upon the Buddhi (intellect) with mind (reflexively), the Param Pada (Brahma) should be obtained. 53.

ख-मध्ये कुरु छात्मानमात्म-मध्ये छ खं कुरु |
सर्वं छ ख-मयं कृत्वा न किंछिदपि छिन्तयेत || ५५ ||

kha-madhye kuru chātmānamātma-madhye cha khaṃ kuru |
sarvaṃ cha kha-mayaṃ kṛtvā na kiṃchidapi chintayet || 55 ||

Keep the âtmâ inside the Kha (Brahma) and place Brahma inside your âtmâ. Having made everything pervaded with Kha (Brahma), think of nothing else. 54.

अन्तः शून्यो बहिः शून्यः शून्यः कुम्भ इवाम्बरे |
अन्तः पूर्णो बहिः पूर्णः पूर्णः कुम्भ इवार्णवे || ५६ ||

antaḥ śūnyo bahiḥ śūnyaḥ śūnyaḥ kumbha ivāmbare |
antaḥ pūrṇo bahiḥ pūrṇaḥ pūrṇaḥ kumbha ivārṇave || 56 ||

One should become void in and void out, and voice like a pot in the space. Full in and full outside, like a jar in the ocean. 55.

बाह्य-छिन्ता न कर्तव्या तथैवान्तर-छिन्तनम |
सर्व-छिन्तां परित्यज्य न किंछिदपि छिन्तयेत || ५७ ||

bāhya-chintā na kartavyā tathaivāntara-chintanam |
sarva-chintāṃ parityajya na kiṃchidapi chintayet || 57 ||

He should be neither of his inside nor of outside world; and, leaving all thoughts, he should think of nothing. 56.

सङ्कल्प-मात्र-कलनैव जगत्समग्रं
सङ्कल्प-मात्र-कलनैव मनो-विलासः |
सङ्कल्प-मात्र-मतिमुत्सृज निर्विकल्पम
आश्रित्य निश्छयमवाप्नुहि राम शान्तिम || ५८ ||

sangkalpa-mātra-kalanaiva jaghatsamaghraṃ
sangkalpa-mātra-kalanaiva mano-vilāsaḥ |
sangkalpa-mātra-matimutsṛja nirvikalpam
āśritya niśchayamavāpnuhi rāma śāntim || 58 ||

The whole of this world and all the schemes of the mind are but the creations of thought. Discarding these thoughts and taking leave of all conjectures, O Râma! obtain peace. 57.

कर्पूरमनले यद्वत्सैन्धवं सलिले यथा ।
तथा सन्धीयमानं छ मनस्तत्त्वे विलीयते ॥ ५९ ॥

karpūramanale yadvatsaindhavaṃ salile yathā ।
tathā sandhīyamānaṃ cha manastattve vilīyate ॥ 59 ॥

As camphor disappears in fire, and rock salt in water, so the mind united with the âtmâ loses its identity. 58.

जज्ञेयं सर्वं परतीतं छ जज्ञानं छ मन उछ्यते ।
जज्ञानं जज्ञेयं समं नष्ह्टं नान्यः पन्था दवितीयकः ॥ ६० ॥

jñeyaṃ sarvaṃ pratītaṃ cha jñānaṃ cha mana uchyate ।
jñānaṃ jñeyaṃ samaṃ naṣhṭaṃ nānyaḥ panthā dvitīyakaḥ ॥ 60 ॥

When the knowable, and the knowledge, are both destroyed equally, then there is no second way (*i.e.*, Duality is destroyed). 59.

मनो-दृश्यमिदं सर्वं यत्किंछित्स-छराछरम ।
मनसो हयुन्मनी-भावाद्द्वैतं नैवोलभ्यते ॥ ६१ ॥

mano-dṝśyamidaṃ sarvaṃ yatkiṃchitsa-charācharam ।
manaso hyunmanī-bhāvāddvaitaṃ naivolabhyate ॥ 61 ॥

All this movable and immovable world is mind. When the mind has attained to the unmanî avasthâ, there is no dwaita (from the absence of the working of the mind.) 60

जज्ञेय-वस्तु-परित्यागाद्विलयं याति मानसम ।
मनसो विलये जाते कैवल्यमवशिष्ह्यते ॥ ६२ ॥

jñeya-vastu-parityāghādvilayaṃ yāti mānasam ।
manaso vilaye jāte kaivalyamavaśiṣhyate ॥ 62 ॥

Mind disappears by removing the knowable, and, on its disappearance, âtmâ only remains behind. 61.

एवं नाना-विधोपायाः सम्यक्स्वानुभवान्विताः ।
समाधि-मार्गाः कथिताः पूर्वाछार्यैर्महात्मभिः ॥ ६३ ॥

evaṃ nānā-vidhopāyāḥ samyaksvānubhavānvitāḥ ।
samādhi-mārghāḥ kathitāḥ pūrvāchāryairmahātmabhiḥ ॥ 63 ॥

The high-souled Âchâryas (Teachers) of yore gained experience in the various methods of Samâdhi themselves, and then they preached them to others. 62.

सुष्हुम्णायै कुण्डलिन्यै सुधायै छन्द्र-जन्मने |
मनोन्मन्यै नमस्तुभ्यं महा-शक्त्यै छिद-आत्मने || ६४ ||

suṣhumṇāyai kuṇḍalinyai sudhāyai chandra-janmane |
manonmanyai namastubhyaṃ mahā-śaktyai chid-ātmane || 64 ||

Salutations to Thee, O Suṣumnâ, to Thee O Kuṇḍalinî, to Thee O Sudhâ, born of Chandra, to Thee O Manomnanî! to Thee O great power, energy and the intelligent spirit. 63.

अशक्य-तत्त्व-बोधानां मूढानामपि संमतम |
परोक्तं गोरक्ह्-नाथेन नादोपासनमुछ्यते || ६५ ||

aśakya-tattva-bodhānāṃ mūḍhānāmapi saṃmatam |
proktaṃ ghorakṣha-nāthena nādopāsanamuchyate || 65 ||

I will describe now the practice of anâhata nâda, as propounded by Gorakṣa Nâtha, for the benefit of those who are unable to understand the principles of knowledge—a method, which is liked by the ignorant also. 64.

शरी-आदिनाथेन स-पाद-कोटि-
लय-परकाराः कथिता जयन्ति |
नादानुसन्धानकमेकमेव
मन्यामहे मुख्यतमं लयानाम || ६६ ||

śrī-ādināthena sa-pāda-koṭi-
laya-prakārāḥ kathitā jayanti |
nādānusandhānakamekameva
manyāmahe mukhyatamaṃ layānām || 66 ||

Âdinâtha propounded 1¼ crore methods of trance, and they are all extant. Of these, the hearing of the anâhata nâda is the Only one, the chief, in my opinion. 65.

मुक्तासने सथितो योगी मुद्रां सन्धाय शाम्भवीम |
शृणुयाद्दक्षिहिणे कर्णे नादमन्तास्थमेकधीः || ६७ ||

muktāsane sthito yoghī mudrāṃ sandhāya śāmbhavīm | śṛṇuyāddakṣhiṇe karṇe nādamantāsthamekadhīḥ || 67 ||

Sitting with Mukta Âsana and with the Sâmbhavî Madill, the Yogî should hear the sound inside his right ear, with collected mind. 66.

शरवण-पुट-नयन-युगल
घराण-मुखानां निरोधनं कार्यम |
शुद्ध-सुष्हुम्णा-सरणौ
सफुटममलः शरूयते नादः || ६८ ||

śravaṇa-puṭa-nayana-yughala
ghrāṇa-mukhānāṃ nirodhanaṃ kāryam |
śuddha-suṣhumṇā-saraṇau
sphuṭamamalaḥ śrūyate nādaḥ || 68 ||

The ears, the eyes, the nose, and the mouth should be closed and then the clear sound is heard in the passage of the Suṣumnâ which has been cleansed of all its impurities. 67.

आरम्भश्छ घटश्छैव तथा परिछयो|अपि छ |
निष्हपत्तिः सर्व-योगेष्हु सयादवस्था-छतुष्हटयम || ६९ ||

ārambhaścha ghaṭaśchaiva tathā parichayo|api cha | niṣhpattiḥ sarva-yogheṣhu syādavasthā-chatuṣhṭayam || 69 ||

In all the Yogas, there are four states: (1) ârambha or the preliminary, (2) Ghata, or the state of a jar, (3) Parichaya (known), (4) niṣpatti (consumate.) 68.

Ârambha Avasthâ.

अथ आरम्भावस्था
बरह्म-गरन्थेर्भवेद्भेदो हयानन्दः शून्य-सम्भवः |
विछित्रः कवणको देहे|अनाहतः शरूयते धवनिः || ७० ||

atha ārambhāvasthā
brahma-ghrantherbhavedbhedo hyānandaḥ śūnya-sambhavaḥ |
vichitraḥ kvaṇako dehe|anāhataḥ śrūyate dhvaniḥ || 70 ||

When the Brahma granthi (in the heart) is pierced through by Prâṇâyâma, then a sort of happiness is experienced in the vacuum of the heart, and the anâhat sounds, like various tinkling sounds of ornaments, are heard in the body. 69.

दिव्य-देहश्छ तेजस्वी दिव्य-गन्धस्त्वरोगवान |
सम्पूर्ण-हृदयः शून्य आरम्भे योगवान्भवेत || ७१ ||

divya-dehaścha tejasvī divya-ghandhastvaroghavān |
sampūrṇa-hṛdayaḥ śūnya ārambhe yoghavānbhavet || 71 ||

In the ârambha, a Yogî's body becomes divine, glowing, healthy, and emits a divine swell. The whole of his heart becomes void. 70.

The Ghata Avasthâ.

अथ घटावस्था
दवितीयायां घटीकृत्य वायुर्भवति मध्यगः |
दृढासनो भवेद्योगी जत्रानी देव-समस्तदा || ७२ ||

atha ghaṭāvasthā
dvitīyāyāṃ ghaṭīkṛtya vāyurbhavati madhyaghaḥ |
dṛḍhāsano bhavedyoghī jñānī deva-samastadā || 72 ||

In the second stage, the airs are united into one and begin moving in the middle channel. The Yogî's posture becomes firm, and he becomes wise like a god. 71.

विष्ह्णु-गरन्थेस्ततो भेदात्परमानन्द-सूछकः |
अतिशून्ये विमर्दश्छ भेरी-शब्दस्तदा भवेत || ७३ ||

viṣhṇu-ghranthestato bhedātparamānanda-sūchakaḥ |
atiśūnye vimardaścha bherī-śabdastadā bhavet || 73 ||

By this means the Viṣṇu knot (in the throat) is pierced which is indicated by highest pleasure experienced, And then the Bherî sound (like the beating of a kettle drain) is evolved in the vacuum in the throat. 72.

The Parichaya Avasthâ.

अथ परिछयावस्था
तृतीयायां तु विज्ञेयो विहायो मर्दल-धवनिः |
महा-शून्यं तदा याति सर्व-सिद्धि-समाश्रयम || ७४ ||

atha parichayāvasthā
tṛtīyāyāṃ tu vijñeyo vihāyo mardala-dhvaniḥ |
mahā-śūnyaṃ tadā yāti sarva-siddhi-samāśrayam || 74 ||

In the third stage, the sound of a drum is known to arise in tie Sûnya between the eyebrows, and then the Vâyu goes to the Mahâśûnya, which is the home of all the siddhîs. 73.

छित्तानन्दं तदा जित्वा सहजानन्द-सम्भवः |
दोष्ह-दुःख-जरा-वयाधि-कष्हुधा-निद्रा-विवर्जितः || ७५ ||

chittānandaṃ tadā jitvā sahajānanda-sambhavaḥ |
doṣha-duḥkha-jarā-vyādhi-kṣhudhā-nidrā-vivarjitaḥ || 75 ||

Conquering, then, the pleasures of the mind, ecstacy is spontaneously produced which is devoid of evils, pains, old age, disease, hunger and sleep. 74.

अथ निष्ह्पत्त्य अवस्था
रुद्र-गरन्थिं यदा भित्त्वा शर्व-पीठ-गतो|अनिलः |
निष्हपत्तौ वैणवः शब्दः कवणद-वीणा-कवणो भवेत || ७६ ||

atha niṣhpatty-avasthā
rudra-ghranthiṃ yadā bhittvā śarva-pīṭha-ghato|anilaḥ |
niṣhpattau vaiṇavaḥ śabdaḥ kvaṇad-vīṇā-kvaṇo bhavet || 76 ||

When the Rudra granthi is pierced and the air enters the seat of the Lord (the space between the eyebrows), then the perfect sound like that of a flute is produced. 75.

एकीभूतं तदा छित्तं राज-योगाभिधानकम |
सृष्हिट-संहार-कर्तासौ योगीश्वर-समो भवेत || ७७ ||

ekībhūtaṃ tadā chittaṃ rāja-yoghābhidhānakam |
sṛṣhṭi-saṃhāra-kartāsau yoghīśvara-samo bhavet || 77 ||

The union of the mind and the sound is called the Râja-Yoga. The (real) Yogî becomes the creator and destroyer of the universe, like God. 76.

अस्तु वा मास्तु वा मुक्तिरत्रैवाखण्डितं सुखम |
लयोद्भवमिदं सौख्यं राज-योगादवाप्यते || ७८ ||

astu vā māstu vā muktiratraivākhaṇḍitaṃ sukham | layodbhavamidaṃ saukhyaṃ rāja-yoghādavāpyate || 78 ||

Perpetual Happiness is achieved by this; I do not care if the mukti be not attained. This happiness, resulting from absorption [in Brahma], is obtained by means of Raja-Yoga. 77.

राज-योगमजानन्तः केवलं हठ-कर्मिणः |
एतानभ्यासिनो मन्ये परयास-फल-वर्जितान || ७९ ||

rāja-yoghamajānantaḥ kevalaṃ haṭha-karmiṇaḥ | etānabhyāsino manye prayāsa-phala-varjitān || 79 ||

Those who are ignorant of the Râja-Yoga and practise only the Haṭha-Yoga, will, in my opinion, waste their energy fruitlessly. 78.

उन्मन्य-अवाप्तये शीघ्रं भरू-धयानं मम संमतम |
राज-योग-पदं पराप्तुं सुखोपायो|अल्प-छेतसाम |
सद्यः परत्यय-सन्धायी जायते नादजो लयः || ८० ||

unmany-avāptaye śīghraṃ bhrū-dhyānaṃ mama saṃmatam | rāja-yogha-padaṃ prāptuṃ sukhopāyo|alpa-chetasām | sadyaḥ pratyaya-sandhāyī jāyate nādajo layaḥ || 80 ||

Contemplation on the space between the eyebrows is, in my opinion, best for accomplishing soon the *Unmanî* state. For people of small intellect, it is a very easy method for obtaining perfection in the Raja-Yoga. The Laya produced by nâda, at once gives experience (of spiritual powers). 79.

नादानुसन्धान-समाधि-भाजां
योगीश्वराणां हृदि वर्धमानम |
आनन्दमेकं वछसामगम्यं
जानाति तं शरी-गुरुनाथ एकः || ८१ ||

nādānusandhāna-samādhi-bhājāṃ yoghīśvarāṇāṃ hṛdi vardhamānam | ānandamekaṃ vachasāmaghamyaṃ jānāti taṃ śrī-ghurunātha ekaḥ || 81 ||

The happiness which increases in the hearts of Yogiśwaras, who have gained success in Samâdhi by means of attention to the nâda, is beyond description, and is known to *Śri Gurû Nâtha* alone. 80.

कर्णौ पिधाय हस्ताभ्यां यः शृणोति धवनिं मुनिः |
तत्र छित्तं सथिरीकुर्यादयावत्स्थिर-पदं वरजेत || ८२ ||

karṇau pidhāya hastābhyāṃ yaḥ śṝṇoti dhvanim muniḥ |
tatra chittaṃ sthirīkuryādyāvatsthira-padaṃ vrajet || 82 ||

The sound which a muni hears by closing his ears with his fingers, should be heard attentively, till the mind becomes steady in it. 81.

अभ्यस्यमानो नादो|अयं बाह्यमावृणुते धवनिम |
पक्ष्हादविक्ष्हेपमखिलं जित्वा योगी सुखी भवेत || ८३ ||

abhyasyamāno nādo|ayaṃ bāhyamāvṝṇute dhvanim |
pakṣhādvikṣhepamakhilaṃ jitvā yoghī sukhī bhavet || 83 ||

By practising with this nâda, all other external sounds are stopped. The Yogî becomes happy by overcoming all distractions within 15 days. 82.

शरूयते परथमाभ्यासे नादो नाना-विधो महान |
ततो|अभ्यासे वर्धमाने शरूयते सूक्ष्हम-सूक्ष्हमकः || ८४ ||

śrūyate prathamābhyāse nādo nānā-vidho mahān |
tato|abhyāse vardhamāne śrūyate sūkṣhma-sūkṣhmakaḥ || 84 ||

In the beginning, the sounds heard are of great variety and very loud; but, as the practice increases, they become more and more subtle. 83.

आदौ जलधि-जीमूत-भेरी-झर्झर-सम्भवाः |
मध्ये मर्दल-शङ्खोत्था घण्टा-काहलजास्तथा || ८५ ||

ādau jaladhi-jīmūta-bherī-jharjhara-sambhavāḥ |
madhye mardala-śangkhotthā ghaṇṭā-kāhalajāstathā || 85 ||

In the first stage, the sounds are surging, thundering like the beating of kettle drums and jingling ones. In the intermediate stage, they are like those produced by conch, *Mridanga*, bells, &c. 84.

अन्ते तु किङ्किणी-वंश-वीणा-भरमर-निःस्वनाः ।
इति नानाविधा नादाः शरूयन्ते देह-मध्यगाः ॥ ८६ ॥

ante tu kingkiṇī-vaṃśa-vīṇā-bhramara-niḥsvanāḥ ।
iti nānāvidhā nādāḥ śrūyante deha-madhyaghāḥ ॥ 86 ॥

In the last stage, the sounds resemble those from tinklets, flute, Vîṇâ, bee, &c. These various kinds of sounds are heard as being produced in the body. 85.

महति शरूयमाणे|अपि मेघ-भेर्य-आदिके धवनौ ।
तत्र सूक्ष्हमात्सूक्ष्हमतरं नादमेव परामृशेत ॥ ८७ ॥

mahati śrūyamāṇe|api megha-bhery-ādike dhvanau ।
tatra sūkṣhmātsūkṣhmataraṃ nādameva parāmṛśet ॥ 87 ॥

Though hearing loud sounds like those of thunder, kettle drums, etc., one should practise with the subtle sounds also. 86.

घनमुत्सृज्य वा सूक्ष्हमे सूक्ष्हममुत्सृज्य वा घने ।
रममाणमपि कष्हिप्तं मनो नान्यत्र छालयेत ॥ ८८ ॥

ghanamutsṛjya vā sūkṣhme sūkṣhmamutsṛjya vā ghane ।
ramamāṇamapi kṣhiptaṃ mano nānyatra chālayet ॥ 88 ॥

Leaving the loudest, taking up the subtle one, and leaving the subtle one, taking up the loudest, thus practising, the distracted mind does not wander elsewhere. 87.

यत्र कुत्रापि वा नादे लगति परथमं मनः ।
तत्रैव सुस्थिरीभूय तेन सार्धं विलीयते ॥ ८९ ॥

yatra kutrāpi vā nāde laghati prathamaṃ manaḥ ।
tatraiva susthirībhūya tena sārdhaṃ vilīyate ॥ 89 ॥

Wherever the mind attaches itself first, it becomes steady there; and then it becomes absorbed in it. 88.

मकरन्दं पिबन्भृङ्गी गन्धं नापेक्ष्हते यथा ।
नादासक्तं तथा छित्तं विष्हयान्नहि काङ्क्ष्हते ॥ ९० ॥

makarandaṃ pibanbhṛngghī ghandhaṃ nāpekṣhate yathā ।
nādāsaktaṃ tathā chittaṃ viṣhayānnahi kāngkṣhate ॥ 90 ॥

Just as a bee, drinking sweet juice, does not care for the smell of the flower; so the mind, absorbed in the nâda, does not desire the objects of enjoyment. 89.

मनो-मत्त-गजेन्द्रस्य विष्हयोद्यान-छारिणः | समर्थो|अयं नियमने निनाद-निशिताङ्कुशः || ९१ ||

mano-matta-ghajendrasya viṣhayodyāna-chāriṇaḥ | samartho|ayaṃ niyamane nināda-niśitāngkuśaḥ || 91 ||

The mind, like an elephant habituated to wander in the garden of enjoyments, is capable of being controlled by the sharp goad of anâhata nâda. 90.

बद्धं तु नाद-बन्धेन मनः सन्त्यक्त-छापलम | परयाति सुतरां सथैर्यं छिन्न-पक्ष्हः खगो यथा || ९२ ||

baddhaṃ tu nāda-bandhena manaḥ santyakta-chāpalam | prayāti sutarāṃ sthairyaṃ chinna-pakṣhaḥ khagho yathā || 92 ||

The mind, captivated in the snare of nâda, gives up all its activity; and, like a bird with clipped wings, becomes calm at once. 91.

सर्व-छिन्तां परित्यज्य सावधानेन छेतसा | नाद एवानुसन्धेयो योग-साम्राज्यमिछ्छता || ९३ ||

sarva-chintāṃ parityajya sāvadhānena chetasā | nāda evānusandheyo yogha-sāmrājyamichchatā || 93 ||

Those desirous of the kingdom of Yoga, should take up the practice of hearing the anâhata nâda, with mind collected and free from all cares. 92.

नादो|अन्तरङ्ग-सारङ्ग-बन्धने वागुरायते | अन्तरङ्ग-कुरङ्गस्य वधे वयाधायते|अपि छ || ९४ ||

nādo|antaranggha-sāranggha-bandhane vāghurāyate | antaranggha-kurangghasya vadhe vyādhāyate|api cha || 94 ||

Nada is the snare for catching the mind; and, when it is caught like a deer, it can be killed also like it. 93.

अन्तरङ्गस्य यमिनो वाजिनः परिघायते ।
नादोपास्ति-रतो नित्यमवधार्या हि योगिना ॥ ९५ ॥

antarangghasya yamino vājinaḥ parighāyate ।
nādopāsti-rato nityamavadhāryā hi yoghinā ॥ 95 ॥

Nâda is the bolt of the stable door for the horse (the minds of the Yogîs). A Yogî should determine to practise constantly in the hearing of the nâda sounds. 94.

बद्धं विमुक्त-छाञ्छल्यं नाद-गन्धक-जारणात ।
मनः-पारदमाप्नोति निरालम्बाख्य-खे|अटनम ॥ ९६ ॥

baddhaṃ vimukta-chāñchalyaṃ nāda-ghandhaka-jāraṇāt ।
manaḥ-pāradamāpnoti nirālambākhya-khe|aṭanam ॥ 96 ॥

Mind gets the properties of calcined mercury. When deprived of its unsteadiness it is calcined, combined with the sulphur of nâda, and then it roams like it in tine supportless âkâśa or Brahma. 95.

नाद-शरवणतः कष्हिप्रमन्तरङ्ग-भुजङ्गमम ।
विस्मृतय सर्वमेकाग्रः कुत्रछिन्नहि धावति ॥ ९७ ॥

nāda-śravaṇataḥ kṣhipramantaranggha-bhujangghamam ।
vismṝtaya sarvamekāghraḥ kutrachinnahi dhāvati ॥ 97 ॥

The mind is like a serpent, forgetting all its unsteadiness by hearing the nâda, it does not run away anywhere. 96.

काष्ह्ठे परवर्तितो वह्निः काष्ह्ठेन सह शाम्यति ।
नादे परवर्तितं छित्तं नादेन सह लीयते ॥ ९८ ॥

kāṣhṭhe pravartito vahniḥ kāṣhṭhena saha śāmyati ।
nāde pravartitaṃ chittaṃ nādena saha līyate ॥ 98 ॥

The fire, catching firewood, is extinguished along with it (after burning it up); and so the mind also, working with the nâda, becomes latent along with it. 97.

घण्टादिनाद-सक्त-सतब्धान्तः-करण-हरिणस्य ।
परहरणमपि सुकरं सयाछछर-सन्धान-परवीणश्छेत ॥ ९९ ॥

ghaṇṭādināda-sakta-stabdhāntaḥ-karaṇa-hariṇasya |
praharaṇamapi sukaraṃ syāchchara-sandhāna-pravīṇaśchet || 99 ||

The antahkaraṇa (mind), like a deer, becomes absorbed and motionless on hearing the sound of hells, etc.; and then it is very easy for an expert archer to kill it. 98.

अनाहतस्य शब्दस्य धवनिर्य उपलभ्यते |
धवनेरन्तर्गतं जञेयं जञेयस्यान्तर्गतं मनः |
मनस्तत्र लयं याति तद्विष्हणोः परमं पदम || १०० ||

anāhatasya śabdasya dhvanirya upalabhyate |
dhvanerantarghataṃ jñeyaṃ jñeyasyāntarghataṃ manaḥ |
manastatra layaṃ yāti tadviṣhṇoḥ paramaṃ padam || 100 ||

The knowable interpenetrates the anâhata sound which is heard, and the mind interpenetrates the knowable. The mind becomes absorbed there, which is the seat of the all-pervading, almighty Lord. 99.

तावदाकाश-सङ्कल्पो यावछछब्दः परवर्तते |
निःशब्दं तत-परं बरह्म परमातेति गीयते || १०१ ||

tāvadākāśa-sangkalpo yāvachchabdaḥ pravartate |
niḥśabdaṃ tat-paraṃ brahma paramāteti ghīyate || 101 ||

So long as the sounds continue, there is the idea of âkâśa. When they disappear, then it is called Para Brahma, Paramâtmana. 100.

यत्किंछिन्नाद-रूपेण शरूयते शक्तिरेव सा |
यस्तत्त्वान्तो निराकारः स एव परमेश्वरः || १०२ ||

yatkiṃchinnāda-rūpeṇa śrūyate śaktireva sā |
yastattvānto nirākāraḥ sa eva parameśvaraḥ || 102 ||

Whatever is heard in the form of nâda, is the śakti (power). That which is formless, the final state of the Tatwas, is tile Parameśwara. 101.

इति नादानुसन्धानम
सर्वे हठ-लयोपाया राजयोगस्य सिद्धये |
राज-योग-समारूढः पुरुष्हः काल-वञ्छकः || १०३ ||

iti nādānusandhānam
sarve haṭha-layopāyā rājayoghasya siddhaye |
rāja-yogha-samārūḍhaḥ puruṣhaḥ kāla-vañchakaḥ || 103 ||

All the methods of Haṭha are meant for gaining success in the Raja-Yoga; for, the man, who is well-established in the Raja-Yoga, overcomes death. 102.

तत्त्वं बीजं हठः कष्हेत्रमौदासीन्यं जलं तरिभिः |
उन्मनी कल्प-लतिका सद्य एव परवर्तते || १०४ ||

tattvaṃ bījaṃ haṭhaḥ kṣhetramaudāsīnyaṃ jalaṃ tribhiḥ |
unmanī kalpa-latikā sadya eva pravartate || 104 ||

Tatwa is the seed, Haṭha the field; and Indifference (Vairâgya) the water. By the action of these three, the creeper Unmanî thrives very rapidly. 103.

सदा नादानुसन्धानात्क्षहीयन्ते पाप-संछयाः |
निरञ्जने विलीयेते निश्छितं छित्त-मारुतौ || १०५ ||

sadā nādānusandhānātkṣhīyante pāpa-saṃchayāḥ |
nirañjane vilīyete niśchitaṃ chitta-mārutau || 105 ||

All the accumulations of sins are destroyed by practising always with the nâda; and the mind and the airs do certainly become latent in the colorless (Paramâtmana). 104.

शङ्ख-दुन्धुभि-नादं छ न शृणोति कदाछन |
काष्हठवज्जायते देह उन्मन्यावस्थया धरुवम || १०६ ||

śangkha-dundhubhi-nādaṃ cha na śṛṇoti kadāchana |
kāṣhṭhavajjāyate deha unmanyāvasthayā dhruvam || 106 ||

Such a one. does not hear the noise of the conch and Dundubhi. Being in the Unmanî avasthâ, his body becomes like a piece of wood. 105.

सर्वावस्था-विनिर्मुक्तः सर्व-छिन्ता-विवर्जितः |
मृतवत्तिष्हठते योगी स मुक्तो नात्र संशयः || १०७ ||

sarvāvasthā-vinirmuktaḥ sarva-chintā-vivarjitaḥ |
mṛtavattiṣhṭhate yoghī sa mukto nātra saṃśayaḥ || 107 ||

There is no doubt, such a Yogî becomes free from all states, from all cares, and remains like one dead. 106.

खाद्यते न छ कालेन बाध्यते न छ कर्मणा |
साध्यते न स केनापि योगी युक्तः समाधिना || १०८ ||

khādyate na cha kālena bādhyate na cha karmaṇā |
sādhyate na sa kenāpi yoghī yuktaḥ samādhinā || 108 ||

He is not devoured by death, is not bound by his actions. The Yogî who is engaged in Samâdhi is overpowered by none. 107.

न गन्धं न रसं रूपं न छ सपर्शं न निःस्वनम |
नात्मानं न परं वेत्ति योगी युक्तः समाधिना || १०९ ||

na ghandhaṃ na rasaṃ rūpaṃ na cha sparśaṃ na niḥsvanam |
nātmānaṃ na paraṃ vetti yoghī yuktaḥ samādhinā || 109 ||

The Yogî, engaged in Samâdhi, feels neither smell, taste, color, touch, sound, nor is conscious of his own self. 108.

छित्तं न सुप्तं नोजाग्रत्स्मृति-विस्मृति-वर्जितम |
न छास्तमेति नोदेति यस्यासौ मुक्त एव सः || ११० ||

chittaṃ na suptaṃ nojāghratsmṝti-vismṝti-varjitam |
na chāstameti nodeti yasyāsau mukta eva saḥ || 110 ||

He whose mind is neither sleeping, waking, remembering, destitute of memory, disappearing nor appearing, is liberated. 109.

न विजानाति शीतोष्ह्णं न दुःखं न सुखं तथा |
न मानं नोपमानं छ योगी युक्तः समाधिना || १११ ||

na vijānāti śītoṣhṇaṃ na duḥkhaṃ na sukhaṃ tathā |
na mānaṃ nopamānaṃ cha yoghī yuktaḥ samādhinā || 111 ||

He feels neither heat, cold, pain, pleasure, respect nor disrespect. Such a Yogî is absorbed in Samâdhi. 110.

सवस्थो जाग्रदवस्थायां सुप्तवद्यो|अवतिष्ह्ठते |
निःश्वासोछ्छ्वास-हीनश्छ निश्छितं मुक्त एव सः || ११२ ||

svastho jāghradavasthāyāṃ suptavadyo|avatiṣhṭhate | niḥśvāsochchvāsa-hīnaścha niśchitaṃ mukta eva saḥ || 112 ||

He who, though awake, appears like one sleeping, and is without inspiration and expiration, is certainly free. 111.

अवध्यः सर्व-शस्त्राणामशक्यः सर्व-देहिनाम |
अग्राह्यो मन्त्र-यन्त्राणां योगी युक्तः समाधिना || ११३ ||

avadhyaḥ sarva-śastrāṇāmaśakyaḥ sarva-dehinām | aghrāhyo mantra-yantrāṇāṃ yoghī yuktaḥ samādhinā || 113 ||

The Yogî, engaged in Samâdhi, cannot be killed by any instrument, and is beyond the controlling power of beings. He is beyond the reach of incantations and charms. 112.

यावद्विदुर्न भवति दृढः पराण-वात-परबन्धात |
यावद्ध्याने सहज-सदृशं जायते नैव तत्त्वं
तावज्ज्ञानं वदति तदिदं दम्भ-मिथ्या-परलापः || ११४ ||

yāvadvidurna bhavati dṛḍhaḥ prāṇa-vāta-prabandhāt | yāvaddhyāne sahaja-sadṛśaṃ jāyate naiva tattvaṃ tāvajjñānaṃ vadati tadidaṃ dambha-mithyā-pralāpaḥ || 114 ||

As long as the Prâṇa does not enter and flow in the middle channel and the *vindu* does not become firm by the control of the movements of the Prâṇa; as long as the mind does not assume the form of Brahma without any effort in contemplation, so long all the talk of knowledge and wisdom is merely the nonsensical babbling of a mad man. 113.

THE END.

इति हठ-योग-परदीपिकायां समाधि-लक्ष्हणं नाम छतुर्थोपदेशः |

iti haṭha-yogha-pradīpikāyāṃ samādhi-lakṣhaṇaṃ nāma chaturthopadeśaḥ |

CPSIA information can be obtained
at www.ICGtesting.com
Printed in the USA
LVHW010240010620
657104LV00021B/1583

9 781463 727918